International
Education
for
Spaceship
Earth

NEW DIMENSIONS SERIES:

SIMULATION GAMES FOR
THE SOCIAL STUDIES CLASSROOM

INTERPRETING
THE NEWSPAPER IN THE CLASSROOM:
FOREIGN NEWS AND WORLD VIEWS

TEACHING THE COMPARATIVE
APPROACH TO AMERICAN STUDIES

INTERNATIONAL EDUCATION
FOR SPACESHIP EARTH

TEACHING ABOUT WAR
AND WAR PREVENTION

International Education for Spaceship Earth

by *David C. King*
for the Foreign Policy Association

The Foreign Policy Association

The Foreign Policy Association is a private, nonprofit, nonpartisan educational organization. Its objective is to stimulate wider interest, greater understanding, and more effective participation by American citizens in world affairs. However, as an organization, it takes no position on issues of United States foreign policy. In its publications the FPA strives to insure factual accuracy, but the opinions expressed are those of the authors and not of the organization.

The New Dimensions series is published under the School Services program of the Foreign Policy Association; its purpose is to suggest ways by which social studies teachers can add "new dimensions" to their teaching, especially about world affairs.

In preparing this book we are grateful for the advice and assistance of Bryant Wedge, M.D., of the Institute for the Study of National Behavior in Princeton, New Jersey; George Comstock, formerly of the Department of Journalism, New York University and now with the RAND Corporation; and Penn T. Kimball and W. Phillips Davison of the Graduate School of Journalism, Columbia University. Also, we should like to thank Howard D. Mehlinger of the University of Indiana, Robin W. Winks of Yale University and Alfred O. Hero of the World Peace Foundation.

Robert S. Riche, Jo Linton and Jack Voelpel provided invaluable editorial and stylistic suggestions. Anthony Cassen of the Blair Summer School of Journalism, Blairstown, New Jersey, and Stewart R. MacDonald of the American Newspaper Publishers Association were most helpful in suggesting materials. For editorial direction and supervision of the series, the Foreign Policy Association thanks David C. King, Editorial Director.

JAMES M. BECKER
DIRECTOR
School Services
Foreign Policy Association

CONTENTS

Introduction

THIS BOOK IS BASED ON AN EXTENSIVE STUDY CONDUCTED BY the Foreign Policy Association for the U.S. Office of Education on needs and priorities in international education. A great many people from all parts of the country, and from a variety of disciplines, participated in the meetings and discussions involved in this effort. The Director of the project was James M. Becker, Director of the School Services Program of FPA, and the Project Coordinator was Professor Lee Anderson of Northwestern University, who also drafted major parts of the project's report. In addition, a number of distinguished scholars contributed portions of the final report, which is titled

An Examination of Objectives, Needs and Priorities in International Education in U.S. Secondary and Elementary Schools. (A list of the individual contributors will be found on pages 131–132.)[1]

For simplicity, this will be referred to as the "Study" or the "Report." And to avoid an excessive number of footnotes, reference to page numbers in the Report will simply be put in parentheses;[2] where outside sources are cited, the conventional form of footnoting will be used.

Although much of what is said here will be directed to the social studies teacher, we would like to emphasize that the concerns of the Study go beyond the artificial limits of traditional course offerings. As Lewis Paul Todd said in a review of the Study in the *Civic Leader*, the title of the Report "would be more accurate if the word 'international' were deleted, for the goals the authors hold before us are immediately relevant to the entire educational process."

We would also like to point out that the views and recommendations presented here are those of the author and the contributors to the Study, and do not necessarily reflect the policies of the Foreign Policy Association.

The last chapter of this book, Readings, presents the views of leading figures in the field of social education, regarding the necessity and manner of expanding and changing the traditional approach of teaching international relations.

---

[1] A number of position papers prepared for the Study appeared in a special issue of *Social Education* titled *International Education for the Twenty-First Century*, XXXII, Nov. 1968.

[2] Copies of the complete Report, in microfiche or hard cover, are available from ERIC Document Reproduction Service, National Cash Register Company, 4936 Fairmount Avenue, Bethesda, Maryland 20014. (Code number ED–031–612.) Prices are $24.60 for hard copy; $2.00 for microfiche.

PART I

A DIGEST
OF THE REPORT

1

The World Was
Discovered in 1969

A FEW CENTURIES AGO, MARCO POLO TRAVELED BY LAND TO the east and a little later Columbus went by sea to the west. As much by accident as by design, their journeys served to tear the European village out of its isolated corner and give Western man fantastic new horizons to explore as well as a different view of the world he lived in. In 1969, three astronauts traveled in a new dimension, outward into space, and allowed us for the first time to get a wholly new perspective on ourselves.

We thought we had a pretty good idea of what these earth portraits taken from the moon were going to look like, but once we actually saw them they created something of a shock. Perhaps we hadn't really expected that the globe would look so small or so frail or so alone—a pretty little blue speck floating helplessly in the immense sea of space. For the people who contributed their time and talents to the Study, the hope is that this new image can help pull us out of our myopic perspective and help teach us to look at the world as a single system.

Now there really isn't much new in this concept of "spaceship earth." For a long time we've been talking about such things as "the shrinking globe" and the "inter-relatedness of man." What is new is the idea that we really have to sit down and think about what this means, which is something we haven't bothered to do. That, in fact, is the major thrust of the Study: if we are going to survive as "riders on the earth together" we have to make some pretty drastic changes in our thinking and in the ways we educate our young people.

No matter how much lip-service we pay to the idea of a global society, most of us still look at the world—and teach our students to look at it—as a patchwork quilt of different pieces belonging to different groups. That view is correct. Partly. But in narrowing our vision to the separate pieces, we don't see how those pieces fit together or what they have in common or how much overlapping there is. In previous generations we didn't have to con-cern ourselves with the total picture. As Robert Harper stated, "throughout most of history mankind did exist in separate, almost isolated cultural islands . . . now most of humanity is part of a single world-wide system." (p. 23)

Of course there were lots of contacts between nations in the past, but usually (unless you were invaded) you could pick and choose those contacts, just as China and Japan chose to close the door on the West, and just as many isolated pockets of humanity didn't even know there was anybody around to lock out. But now the global village is impressed upon us every day in hundreds of ways and we have to learn to live with it whether we want to or not. The tourist with his camera and Palm Beach shirt, the Venezuelan laborer drinking a Coke, a U.N. debate involving 126 nations, a Moscow teenager in denims and beads, an international convention of physicists, a farmer in India planting a new strain of Mexican wheat developed by an American foundation—these all suggest some of the myriad forms of contact that cross national boundaries. What we are witnessing is a "profound change in the human condition"—the world is being transformed from a "*collection* of many lands and peoples to a system of many lands and peoples." (p. 22)

Barbara Ward pictures the emerging world system this way:

> Most of the energies of our society tend towards unity—the energy of Science and technological change, the energy of curiosity and research, of self-interest and economics, the energy—in many ways the most violent of them all—the energy of potential aggression and destruction. We have become neighbors in terms of inescapable proximity and instant communication. We are neighbors in economic interest and technological direction. We are neighbors in the risk of total destruction.
>
> Barbara Ward, *Spaceship Earth* (Columbia U. Press, 1966) p. 14; quoted in the Report, p. 24.

We say we are aware of this, that we know we live in a world system of continuing revolutionary change, but our actions suggest that the message hasn't really registered. Perhaps nowhere is this failure to comprehend more painfully clear than in the way we teach our young.

Education has always been a conservative force, more concerned with the preservation of past values than with the exploration of future alternatives. That didn't matter much in the past—in fact it served to maintain a certain cultural continuity. But now the gap between the real world and the world we teach about in our schools has become so wide that much of what we teach has become practically meaningless. Perhaps the younger generation has leaped ahead of the older in this regard. As Herbert Kelman stated, "Among the youth of all nations . . . a common universal culture, with a common set of values and tastes, seems to be taking shape." (p. 343) It is no longer surprising to find a youth who feels a closer emotional identification with a peasant in Southeast Asia than with the older generation in his own family. This growing gap led Kenneth Boulding to conclude: "Some of the current revolt of youth, especially of students, may very well be related to the fact that the pablum which they get in primary and secondary schools is so unrelated to the realities of the world today that it produces vomit rather than nourishment." (p. 55)

In the past decade or so, we have made attempts to correct the parochial nature of our social studies teaching. Traditionally these efforts took the form of "current events" units, patchwork affairs that were usually inserted into leftover time slots, like Friday afternoons when the teacher couldn't accomplish much anyhow. A more recent innovation has been "area studies," where the students are exposed to a number of cultures "in depth." Neither of these approaches is adequate. The current events approach fails because it is "in the context of U.S. foreign policy on certain issues of great concern to the United States. This gives students a view of the world as perceived from a nation—a very large one." (p. 308) And the rationale for area studies seems to be to grant "equal time" to non-western cultures, but usually only serves to reinforce the impression of the world as separate patches of real estate.

A major difficulty with both these approaches is that

they prevent the student from seeing the world as a *system*, because he is concentrating only on the individual parts. Lee Anderson asks us to "imagine a child whose knowledge of fruit is confined to experience with apples and oranges. Out of this experience the child develops a concept of fruit, but the concept will be limited because his experience with fruit is limited." (p. 33) He needs a larger conceptual framework for the things he calls fruit. In the same way, students must be helped to grasp the meaning of the global system and how the individual pieces of that system (including its many sub-systems) are interrelated.

What the Study is saying, in other words, is that what we need is *not* a greater proliferation of culture studies or units examining various events in the traditional relations of nation-states. To give students adequate preparation for today's world, the schools must help them to gain a global perspective; that is a difficult idea to get used to and one that is even more difficult to implement. Many of the obstacles are discussed more fully in Chapter 3 of this section, but for the moment, let's just think about one —the idea many have that studying the world system must somehow lead to an over-simplified, idealistic, one-world picture.

This does not have to be the case, and teachers do not have to fear that they must start teaching about the breakdown of the nation-state system and the imminence of some form of world government. What is needed instead is the ability to look both at the patches on the quilt and also to see the quilt itself. Robert Harper, for example, writes about the need to focus on two systems: one, the locally based culture system; the other, the interconnected system. "In the Congo," Harper states, "most people may still live in the locally-based system focused on their own piece of earth real-estate, but Leopoldville is a city with regular communication and traffic with the world-wide network . . . Mexico is both Mexico City, with its rather important position in the interconnected world, and the Indian village, that is only peripherally tied to the world beyond walking distance from the village." (p. 330) Students—and adults for that matter— must gain knowledge and understanding of *both* systems as systems.

Harper's conclusions are reinforced by other contributors to the Study. Chadwick Alger argues that "a way must be found to put . . . issues in the context of the whole. This will require a curriculum that views the total system—not only from a vantage point outside of a specific nation but also from a vantage point outside the nation system itself." (p. 308) And Boulding states that it is "very important . . . for the teachers and researchers in the international system to have an image of the future which does not necessarily involve either total catastrophe, or a reversal of the developmental process, or the destruction of existing national states and their absorption into a universal world culture and polity. . . . We ought to be able to see in the international system that a system is possible which both preserves the national state and is capable of stable peace." (p. 321)

Leften Stavrianos sums up the sort of world view students must have from the point of view of history:

> It means the perspective of an observer perched on the moon rather than ensconced in London or Paris or Washington. It means that for every period of history, we are interested in events and movements of global rather than regional or national significance. More specifically, it means the realization that in the classical period Han China was the equal of the Roman Empire in every respect; that in the medieval period the Mongols were infinitely more significant than the Magna Carta; that in early modern times Russia's expansion

overland and Western Europe's expansion overseas were likewise more noteworthy than the Reformation or the Wars of Religion; and that today the globally significant developments have to do not with Cold War blocs and crises but rather with the passing of Western hegemony and the reversion to the traditional autonomy of the regions of the world.

Leften Stavrianos, "A Global Perspective in the Organization of World History," in *New Perspectives in World History,* The 34th Yearbook of the National Council for the Social Studies, Washington, D.C., 1964; quoted in the Report, p. 85.

Not only must students gain this global perspective, but they must also be equipped to live in a world of constant and rapid change. It has become quite popular to make predictions and projections about the future, but about the only thing these prophecies have in common is that the world of the future will be a rapidly changing one. Bruce Russett put the matter this way:

At this time it is too soon to know just what kind of system will emerge, or even if the situation will, in the near future, stabilize enough for us even to be fully aware that we have a new system. But we do know that it is changing . . . We can be quite sure that it will be a world system in which all people will be much more closely involved than ever before . . . 'One World' has a meaning beyond the understanding even of those who lived just a generation ago.

Bruce Russett, *Trends in World Politics* (Macmillan, 1965) p. 165; quoted in the Report, p. 24.

In terms of education, change must be recognized as a constant and inescapable fact, and education itself must be flexible enough to keep on changing. So far we have not given the proper response to this factor. As Alger points out, ". . . familiarity with a few statistics on change is one thing and adequate response is quite another. International education curriculum has not yet adequately taken into account the potential consequences for the United States, and for the nation system itself, of dramatic changes in population, transportation, and the destructive power of weapons." (p. 309)

What sort of education is required for this rising generation, a generation which will spend much of its adulthood in the twenty-first century? What can and should the schools do? What types of research and teacher training are needed? Are we capable of change? What sort of strategy should we follow? These questions are the subjects of the sections which follow.

BIBLIOGRAPHY

Anderson, Lee and James Becker, "Riders on the Earth Together," *American Education*, May, 1969, pp. 2–4.

Bell, Daniel (ed.), *Toward the Year 2000: Work in Progress* (Boston, Beacon Press, 1969).

Boulding, Kenneth, *The Meaning of the Twentieth Century: The Great Transformation* (New York, Harper & Row, 1965).

Fisher, Roger, *International Conflict for Beginners* (New York, Harper & Row, 1969).

Fuller, R. Buckminster, *Operational Manual for Spaceship Earth* (Southern Illinois University Press, 1969).

"International Education for the Twenty-First Century," *Social Education*, special issue, XXXII, Nov., 1968.

Lasswell, Harold D., "Multiple Loyalties in a Shrinking World," Address to the National Council for the Social Studies Convention, Washington, D.C., November, 1968.

Manning, C. A. W., *The Nature of International Society* (John Wiley & Sons, Inc., 1962).

Pearson, Lester B., "Beyond the Nation Slate," *Saturday Review*, Feb. 15, 1969, p. 24.

Russett, Bruce, *Trends in World Politics* (New York, The Macmillan Co., 1965).

Ward, Barbara, *Spaceship Earth* (New York, Columbia University Press, 1966).

2

Educational Needs
for Spaceship Earth

In trying to pin down just what we mean by "international education" we run into some semantic difficulties.
The term itself is not a happy one. The word "international" reinforces our concept of a world splintered into
separate pieces of real-estate, and it also tends to become
a ". . . giant trashcan in which some place everything
that goes on outside their nation . . . it encompasses so
much that it virtually means nothing at all." (p. 308) Not
surprisingly, one of the major concerns of the Study was
to develop a definition of international education that
could be used as a frame of reference.

One of the important conclusions in this search for a

workable definition was the idea that international education should not be "education bounded." As Leonard Kenworthy points out, no specific discipline or body of subject matter comprises our international concerns. All subjects in both the physical and social sciences impinge on
the international realm. It is important to remember, too,
that ". . . the 'education' in international education is
something that takes place in the total life space of the
individual rather than simply in school classrooms."
(p. 19)

Definition

In its simplest terms, the definition eventually arrived
at was that international education should be considered
as "education about international or global society, as a
whole and in its parts." In more formal terms, the definition is: "the social experience and the learning process
through which individuals acquire and change their images of the world perceived as a totality and their orientation toward particular components of the world system." (p. 30)

What this means for education is that schools must help
children and young people to develop an "international
understanding"; and not an international understanding
in the way we have traditionally used it—the sort of
strange-lands-and-friendly-people approach. Instead, the
implication is that students must be led toward an understanding of the world as a *single unit* so that the schools
will be, in effect, "transmitting to the next generation a
rich image of the 'total earth.'" (p. 71)

It is important to remember that this understanding of
the world system is not something that can be achieved
at a certain point in the individual's experience—it is
rather an on-going, life-long process of learning to look
at events in a certain way. The Study concluded that there
were three general contributions that the curriculum
should make to this understanding: one, an understanding

of the earth as a planet; two, an understanding of mankind as one species of life; and three, an understanding of the international system as one level of human social organization.

An "earth portrait" taken from Apollo 10
Photo Credit: NASA

That raises the question of how we can determine what ought to be selected out and taught from the ever-increasing wealth of information available to us. One way of getting at the question is to try to understand what sorts of skills and information the "world citizen" ought to have. Bruce Joyce looked at this from the perspective of the social sciences:

Geographically it means that he (the student) sees the network of world interdependence and influence. He learns that the exploitation and conservation of resources is not simply a local or regional affair, but a global affair as well. Economically he sees not only the processes of community and national economic interchange, but the networks of international interchange as well, and perhaps more critical, the moral and practical consequences of the actions of man everywhere on man everywhere else . . . Anthropologically our young citizen begins to see interplay of the earth's cultures. He notes the processes of cultural conflict and interchange. He sees too the gradual formation of world culture . . . Sociologically he sees the processes of assimilation and accommodation in the institutions and behavior patterns of the people around him, and he is able to identify the processes by which people are absorbed into the perspectives of their time and place and the processes by which this time of theirs socializes them to the global. Historically, our citizen sees the sweep of time as peoples all over the world have formed and reformed their heritages; mingled them, suppressed them, and found identity in them. (p. 333)

One might argue that this call for a global view, while not utopian in the old world-federation sense, still presents an idealized view of the world. The globe *is*, after all, splintered into more than 130 different national territories; the nation-state *is* the highest secular authority in most matters and anything we do must take these facts into account.

Before we go any further, we should try to deal with that argument.

In the first place, the stress on a global view is not intended to mean that we ignore the nation-state system, but rather that we redress the present imbalance of our view of world affairs. It is certainly useful to examine international issues from the point of view of American or any other nation's foreign policy, but the analysis should not be *only* from that perspective, which tends to reinforce the ethnocentric we-they view. As Alger stated, " 'We' may be different but students tend not to be encouraged to take an analytic posture that will enable them to find out for sure." (p. 310) The student does not learn to look at America's role in the world objectively.

Secondly, the magnitude and complexity of our problems suggests that learning to look at the world as a single system may be essential if we are ever going to find solutions. The danger of nuclear war, of course, threatens everyone, but even if we avoid that threat, more insidious forms of deterioration and destruction may lead to disaster unless we learn to remove our analytic blinders and take the necessary actions. We have all become aware, for example, of the danger posed by the population explosion, and the enlightened citizen can rattle off a string of morbid statistics. But in terms of action, we still operate as though the problem exists "out there" someplace and doesn't really affect us as individuals or as global citizens. This problem alone should be enough to convince us to take a global approach, but when you combine it with the rapid dissipation of our resources, not the least important of which are clean water and air, one wonders how long we can indulge ourselves in the luxury of parochial complacency. As Robert North stated, "The candle of the good life is melting away at both ends." (p. 393)

The development of a global perspective, then, is a pragmatic thing. It does not have to involve intricate theories or affect the loyalty of the citizen to his nation. Instead, it means developing citizens who are capable of looking beyond the nation-state for the solution of certain problems. Kelman presented the argument this way:

> . . . There are many functions which, by their inherent nature and by the nature of the modern world, cannot be properly met by the sovereign nation-state. The ideology of the nation-state, however, erects barriers to supranational or transnational patterns of organization for these functions. The organization of the world in terms of nation-states has such a powerful hold on our thinking that it is almost impossible to conceive it in different terms. (p. 354)

According to the definition of the Study, international education is not designed to foster a sense of world citizenship that competes with the nation-state for the individual's loyalty, but to develop citizens who are capable of seeing that the nation is not the *only* "basis of organizing to carry out the functions of society." (p. 355)

A good illustration of how we can operate with a global outlook is offered by the amazing growth in recent years of multi-national businesses. These global corporations—which have moved far from our stereotype of exploitive companies preying on the naivete of foreign populations—now have a combined production that "exceeds that of all national markets except those of the United States and Russia"; and, at present growth rates, by the end of the century, "the world economy will be more than half-internationalized." [1] What is it that has led businessmen to such enormous extra-national growth, an expansion that is now being referred to as "the new industrial revolution"? The rationale was not supplied by visions of a global society or the loss of ties with one's home nation. Instead, it has been a natural pattern of growth as industries have sought new resources and markets. In the business world, where needs can be filled

---

[1] Polk, Judd, "The Rise of World Corporations," *Saturday Review*, Nov. 22, 1969, pp. 32–33.

by crossing national boundaries, those boundaries are crossed. Our search for solutions to such problems as the growing gap between food production and population growth, between rich and poor, as well as problems of ecology and urbanization, can be better explored if we are armed with a ". . . transnational definition of the world, because such a definition is instrumental to meeting specific needs and interests that have personal significance." (p. 357)

Those of us involved in education should be willing to recognize the fact that so far our efforts to develop citizens with some sense of the world in which they live have largely failed. Charles McClelland reminds us that studies of college and high school graduates show that ". . . attitudes held toward other countries and toward international problems and relations have been found to be primitive, superficial, and highly stereotyped. . . . They do not recall the details of history and geography, among other things, and they leave the impression that they were never exposed to such materials. . . ." (p. 363)

On the basis of what we have said so far, it should be possible to itemize some of the goals international education should strive for:[2]

1. A curriculum that will give students the ability to look at the world as a "planet-wide society," one of a number of types of human societies. (p. 30)

2. The teaching of a set of skills that will enable the individual to learn inside and outside of school and to continue learning after formal education is concluded.

3. The development of programs that "avoid the ethno-

---

[2] These goals are not developed in the Report precisely in this fashion. This listing is merely an attempt to summarize some of the ideas developed by Lee Anderson and James Becker in Chapters I and II of the Report, pp. 16–110.

centrism inherent in sharp divisions between the study of American and non-American societies." (p. 64)

4. The integration of international studies with the trends and discoveries of other disciplines.

5. A curriculum that stresses the interrelatedness of man rather than simply cataloguing points of difference or uniqueness.

6. A curriculum that is oriented toward the exploration of future alternatives.

7. The selection of subject matter and methods that are relevant for people who will be living in a global society that will be characterized by change, ambiguity, growing interrelatedness and continued conflict.

With these criteria in mind, let's try to see what they mean for the educational system.

First, it is safe to say that there is no single plan that can or should be imposed upon the schools, even if this were desirable. Instead, what we need is a large pool of teaching materials and strategies that will allow teachers and students to select information and approaches desired. One of the sets of skills schools should be concerned with is "information processing," rather than trying to compete with other sources as dispensers of information. Students should be learning skills of analysis rather than trying to commit to memory giant chunks of data. McClelland points out that if the selection of information is already made for the students—which is our normal approach—he will never develop the skills to select.

Second, and this really follows from the first point, there should be a heavy emphasis on inquiry learning. The analytic tools acquired through such an approach will help the student to learn intelligently on his own and to deal with such things as ambiguity, change, conflict, and the constant bombardment of data from the mass media. McClelland's argument for this type of learning is worth quoting at some length:

> Most of our teaching from the first grade through the undergraduate college years has concentrated on the setting forth of descriptive details, the specifying of numerous definitions and classifications of data, and the presenting of common sense maxims, principles, and generalities . . . We need to face the interpretation that when college graduates act as illiterates in history and geography after years of teaching in these fields, the reason has to be that the material was not relevant—it did not fit somehow in the cognitive framework. Having failed to gain a foothold it could not grow there. . . .
>
> The task of education in broadening, sharpening, and disciplining the student's 'map of the social world' becomes largely that of developing skills and insights in information selection and information processing. . . . More and more, contemporary man is becoming an information processor. Increasingly, his survival depends on his effectiveness in discriminating among messages arising from distant sources and on his capacity to make decisions about how and when to respond to the incoming information. (pp. 364, 368)

Such learning envisions a different role for both student and teacher. It requires the student to become a more active learner—developing hypotheses, examining evidence, arriving at generalizations. Rather than providing answers or simply lecturing, the teacher would guide the student in his selection of information and in his methods of inquiry.

 Third, there needs to be a greater concentration on comparative studies, something that has been practically ignored up to now. For a variety of reasons we cannot go into here, our approach to our own history has been one which reinforces a constricted, nationalistic view of our past and our role in the world today. As Howard Meh-linger points out, ". . . treating U.S. history as *only* a unique experience prevents a student from recognizing that in general, and often more fundamental ways, the history of his nation is very similar to that of other nations." (p. 379) The process of socialization does enough to teach about differences among peoples; a good deal of egocentrism and ethnocentrism will be removed if the student learns to look at similarities as well.

A comparative approach means that the student learns to look at man's history as the experience of man as a single species. The frontiers of global history would be pushed farther back in time, and the students would learn something of what the archaeologists and anthropologists have learned about man's development. The agricultural revolution, the rise of civilizations, religion, the development of nation-states, conflict, modernization—all would be seen within the framework of man's common experiences. Instead of learning only about what makes one group of people different from another, the emphasis would also be on shared experiences. This approach requires the analytic tools of inquiry and necessitates a large enough sampling for adequate comparison. For example, the Report states: ". . . in looking at nations in the modern world, a sample that included only the United States and the Soviet Union might lead observers to emphasize the differences between the two societies and to play down the similarities. But were the sample expanded to include Chad, Burma, Haiti and India, an observer might conclude that the U.S. and the U.S.S.R. . . . are very much alike in many respects." (p. 86)

A fourth implication of the Study's view of international education is that learning about the international system must be approached much earlier in the curriculum than has been true in the past. We are beginning to learn some-

thing about the process of socialization, although the surface has barely been scratched. In any case, there is
enough evidence available to conclude that ". . . the elementary years are critical in the formation of many social
values, attitudes and cognitions." (p. 170) The elements
that "socialize" the child, of course, are not limited to the
schools, but apparently what happens is that the school
experience develops a number of important attitudes
toward people who are perceived as different and reinforces others learned from other sources. This means, for
example, that a good portion of the attitudes toward one's
nation are developed early during the school years, while
other attitudes, such as racial prejudice, are reinforced in
school. In other words, the child's basic attitudes, con-
ceptions, and beliefs are developed prior to high school,
and "the elementary school plays the largest part in teaching . . . about the operation of the political system."
(p. 170)

We have always assumed that a child's geography of
awareness develops from things near to him and gradually extends outward to more distant objects. Studies have
shown that this is not the case; children very early develop something of a world view. McClelland states that
". . . the cognitive structure of even the very young
child now includes some national, international, global,
and extra-global elements if from no other source than
television programming." (p. 364) The traditional curriculum has not taken this into account. Even when elements of a world view are grafted onto the high school
years, the effort does little to change the basic attitudes
developed earlier. A number of studies agree with the
findings of Hess and Torney, who concluded: "The result
of these testing sessions failed to support the hypothesis
that significant major development and change occurs
during the high school years. On the contrary, the find-

ings revealed that an unexpected degree of political learn-ing experience had occurred at the pre-high school level." (p. 160)

There is still a great deal to be learned about the inter-national orientation of children and young people. We don't know what sort of world views are developed in the precollege years. For example: "How do third grad-ers 'typically' view war? How do ninth graders view the nation-state system? What images of Africa prevail among primary grade children? How much awareness and knowledge do graduating seniors have of international organization?" (p. 222) These questions suggest some of the many areas where more research is needed. We have to find out what the students' world views are, how they are acquired, how and when they change, and how more constructive views can be developed through the cur-riculum.

Still another implication of the Study's approach to international education is the idea that "World affairs education ought not to be conceived as some kind of compartment that is special and separate." (p. 364) In other words, the development of a global perspective should emerge from the total curriculum, rather than sim-ply from those social studies courses that we traditionally would think had international content.

These goals and implications of the Study have been translated and formalized into a typology of objectives that can serve to guide curriculum development. It would be impossible to describe and examine all of these ob-jectives here, but it might be useful to list the major ones and to follow each with an example of the sort of learning that should take place to achieve those objectives:[3]

[3] A more thorough development of these objectives is in Chapter II of the Report as well as in the *Summary of Needs and Recom-mendations*.

1. An understanding of the world system, which would include the following:

a. Enough knowledge of geology, geography, and astronomy to understand the world as a planet.

b. An understanding of mankind as a species of life; man-other animal comparisons; biological and sociological commonalities and diversities.

c. An understanding of the international or global social system as *one* level of human social organization. Examples: studies of the inter-nation system, cross-national organizations and businesses, war, trade, communication, and major international social phenomena.

2. Development of skills of comparison, analysis, inquiry, and the capacity to make rational judgments. Example: the development of modes of thinking that are relatively free from stereotypic, egocentric, and ethnocentric perceptions.

3. The ability to understand, analyze and judge foreign policy decisions. Example: study units dealing with *how* foreign policy decisions are made.

4. The capacity to observe intelligently and critically, current history of the world system. Example: learning how to deal with the flow of information from the mass media.

5. The ability to adapt to "the realities of the human condition." Example: learning to accept diversity and change, and emotionally to tolerate "the tensions of continued intergroup conflict and hostility."

Even a superficial glance at these objectives makes it clear that the Study is aimed toward a thorough revision of the curriculum, especially in social studies, but with considerable spilling over into other curricular areas as well. Such a revolution in curriculum obviously cannot be created with much speed, if indeed our educational system is capable of such great change. But we cannot afford a generation lag while teachers are trained and curricula are revised before we begin giving our students a more adequate preparation for living in this world. Some things have to be done now. The next chapter will focus on some of the obstacles to change described in the Report, and in Part II we will outline some innovations which seem consistent with the guidelines indicated by the Study.

BIBLIOGRAPHY

Note: As indicated in the Introduction, many of the position papers prepared for the Study appeared in the special issue of *Social Education*, XXXII, Nov., 1968.

Angell, Robert C., "The Growth of Transnational Participation," *Journal of Social Issues*, 23, 1967, p. 108.

Becker, James and Howard Mehlinger (eds.), *International Dimensions in the Social Studies* (Washington, D.C., 38th Yearbook of the National Council for the Social Studies, 1968).

Becker, James and Martha J. Porter, "What Is Education for International Understanding," *Social Education*, XXX, Jan., 1966, p. 31.

Cousins, Norman, "Needed: A New World Theme Song," *Saturday Review*, July, 1968, p. 20.

Easton, David and J. Dennis, *Political Socialization of the Elementary School Child* (Washington, D.C., 36th Yearbook of the National Council for the Social Studies, 1966).

Joyce, Bruce R., *Strategies for Elementary Social Science Education* (Chicago, Science Research Associates, 1965).

Kenworthy, Leonard, "Developing World-Minded Teachers," in Anderson, Howard R. (ed.), *Approaches to an Understanding of World Affairs* (Washington, D.C., 25th Yearbook of the National Council for the Social Studies, 1955).

Long, Harold and Robert King, *Improving the Teaching of World Affairs; The Glens Falls Story,* Bulletin No. 15 (Washington, D.C., The National Council for the Social Studies, 1964).

Moore, Wilbert E., "Global Sociology: The World as a Singular System," in Moore (ed.), *Order and Change: Essays in Comparative Sociology* (N.Y., John Wiley & Sons, 1967).

Patrick, John, *Political Socialization of American Youth* (Bloomington, Ind., Indiana University Press, 1967).

Rogers, Vincent R., "Ethnocentrism and the Social Studies," *Phi Delta Kappan,* XLIX, Dec., 1967, p. 209.

Stavrianos, Leften, "A Global Perspective in the Organization of World History," in *New Perspectives in World History* (Washington, D.C., 34th Yearbook of the National Council for the Social Studies, 1964).

Taylor, Harold, *The World and the American Teacher* (Washington, D.C., American Association of Colleges for Teacher Education, 1967).

Whitehead, Alfred North, *The Aims of Education* (N.Y., The Macmillan Co., 1959).

3

Some Obstacles
to Change

Formal schooling is still but a pale reflection of the pulsating drama of life. In large measure, the school . . . continues to be both insular and insulated; circumscribed by narrow vision and protected by tradition and circumstance from the challenging and dynamic forces of social interaction in the world. (p. 233)

SCHOOLS ARE PRETTY MUCH WHAT WE WANT THEM TO BE, and evidently there is a consensus in this country that schools ought to remain as they are pictured in the above quotation. In other words, the major obstacle to change may be that we simply don't want it.

One reason that we are satisfied with maintaining the *status quo* in our educational system is that any basic change, especially in the area of international education, seems threatening and dangerous. Boulding offers the following thought on this problem:

> Wherever the curriculum of formal education im-
> pinges on images of the world which the local culture
> around it treasures, sensitive areas are set up which are
> avoided as far as possible. Religion, race, and national-
> ism . . . are among these areas, and the study of the
> international system inevitably impinges on all of them.
> It is not surprising therefore that international education
> tends to follow the innocuous patterns of interesting
> stories about strange children, and any attempt to teach
> the international system as a total system might easily
> run into very serious criticism from the defenders of the
> local culture. (p. 318)

Our schools offer what it is safe to offer. Taboo areas
might not be spelled out as such but they are understood
and avoided. As Harper stated, "Any curricular effort
needs to anticipate that world affairs, foreign policy, and
the perspectives of world citizenship will be unfamiliar
intruders in the elementary school world, and far from
familiar acquaintances in the secondary school." (p. 335)

We want our schools to create good American citizens
—patriotic, loyal, and dedicated. As long as our own view
of the world is based on a narrow, nationalistic approach
to world affairs, our educational system will reflect that
view. John Patrick's research led to the conclusion that:
"the schools reinforce and develop strong attitudes toward state and nation. Most children learn well the lessons of conforming to the socio-political *status quo*."
(p. 237)

This desire to avoid change places the teacher in a
difficult position. He is, in Joyce's words, a "surrogate of
the national society," and as such there are few rewards
for him if he attempts to teach something that might be
construed as dangerous or unpatriotic. (p. 335) For many
teachers this means knowingly presenting a lopsided
view of the world, and being aware too that their students

aren't buying it. Boulding states that the teacher is forced to walk a tightrope: ". . . the educator who does not 'tell it like it is' is in great danger of being found out, if the image of the world which he is propagating to his students does not correspond to what they are going to discover in their subsequent life experience." (p. 319)

Even if a teacher does desire innovation, as Irwin T. Sanders writes, this is of "little effect if their supervisors, school administrators, and school boards are not interested in such innovation." [1] The teacher who wants to survive in his profession learns to play it safe. He accepts his role as a "bureaucratic functionary" and eventually develops the capacity to "resist innovative demands, like most professionals in bureaucratic organizations." (p. 257)

The major problem, then, is basic to our educational system; it deals, in fact, with our philosophy of what education is and ought to be. Contributors to the Study focused on other barriers to change, many of which are related to the central problem of attitude just discussed. For the sake of simplicity and brevity, these obstacles can be outlined.

Curriculum Materials

Notable innovations are being developed by a number of curriculum projects, some of which will be mentioned in the next chapter, but on the whole there are few materials available for presenting a global view, particularly in the elementary grades. Joyce concluded: "The situation is so severe in the lower grades that any decent exploration of global perspective is seriously disadvantaged

[1] Sanders, Irwin T., *Professional Education for World Responsibility*, N.Y., Education & World Affairs, Occasional Paper No. 7, 1969, p. 17; quoted in the Report, p. 243.

and this characterization remains essentially true in the high school except for the academically talented students." (p. 336)

Problems of Communication

A communications gap was found to exist on two levels. First, the teacher in the classroom frequently seems to be cut off from innovations that are being developed, particularly by the curriculum projects. H. Thomas Collins concludes that "with the exception of a few materials that publishers have already made available, teachers know very little about the objectives or materials produced by curriculum development centers throughout the country. About all they know is that 'the Projects' do exist 'somewhere,' doing 'something' that 'somehow' is supposed to help them do a better job." (p. 128)

The second area in which a breakdown of communication was found was between scholarly research and the classroom teacher. University scholars, for example, have developed exciting new approaches to American studies by using a comparative approach, but practically none of this scholarship has filtered down to the schools. Frank Klassen argues that colleges and universities produce either scholars or classroom teachers, "leaving a gap exactly in the middle of the whole educational system." (p. 238)

Inability to Think About the Future

Alger mentions two difficulties in this connection. First:

> Education can liberate or imprison. Much that is called international education is of the latter kind. Images of the world of the past and preoccupation with

certain current events filter out much of the world of the present. This almost makes it impossible to think about the future. (p. 308)

His second point is that, if we do try to consider the international system, we tend to think in idealistic terms of a more perfect global society. "The way we talk about 'rule of law' and 'world government,'" he states, "reveals a tragic inability to apply available knowledge to significant international problems and inhibits effective planning for the future." (p. 308)

Boulding also discussed the misconception that looking at the world as a system must inevitably move us in the direction of some sort of world government and "the destruction of existing national sovereignty." We respond to this idea with fear; we do not, by and large, want our world to move in that direction. Boulding concludes that "this is related to the largely subconscious fear that any discussion of religion will lead to the loss of faith or any discussion of race will lead to racial mixtures. All these fears are deeply ingrained in the folk cultures of this country and furthermore they cannot be dismissed as irrational, although they all have strong irrational elements in them." (p. 321)

Our Approach to World Issues

As we have stated earlier, there is a strong tendency for us to think of world affairs matters solely from the perspective of American foreign policy. We are not able to place these issues in a larger, global framework, and so we receive "only a partial view of the world." (p. 308) Alger states, "because the United States is a big nation, and a super power, its citizens and educators have particular difficulty in seeing the total international system with perspective." (p. 308) This difficulty is compounded by another factor: "The strong moral tone of United States foreign policy objectives appears to generate an extreme self-righteousness that inhibits detached evaluation of U.S. performance by its citizens." (p. 310)

Lack of Knowledge

Not only do we have to cope with the emotional content of change, but we must also develop a structure or method of inquiry for the field, and there are important substantive areas where research and exploration are needed. Boulding points out that "It is very hard to teach what we do not know and the awful truth is that we do not know very much about the international system." (p. 320) And Collins presents the idea this way: "In spite of what the assigned curriculum guides may say about the world, it must always be remembered that few teachers teaching today are informed enough about the many complexities of global society to feel secure in designing and carrying out their own individual lessons and courses of study." (p. 117)

Teacher Training

As we do develop bodies of information and methods for teaching a world view to students, there remains the problem of training teachers. The question is raised, "when we have something to teach, who will teach the teachers? This perhaps is a one-generation lag which we can very ill afford." (p. 321) How far we have to go in this regard is revealed by a single, striking statistic produced by a survey conducted by the American Association of Colleges for Teacher Education. The study found, Harold Taylor reports, that "not more than 3 to 5 percent of all teachers have had in the course of their preparation to become teachers in the social sciences or any other area of the curriculum any formal study of cultures other than in the West, or have studied in a field which could properly be described as world affairs." [2]

A survey of these obstacles—and there are others we haven't touched on—can lead to a pretty pessimistic view of the prospects for change. One writer felt the situation to be so grave that ". . . at present, significant overall changes and progress seem highly unlikely if not impossible." (p. 260)

In terms of long-range, sweeping reforms, it is hard to be anything but pessimistic. Such changes are not likely to come about from within the system. The impetus has to be provided by something like the change in opinion created by the first Sputnik—people then became alarmed enough about our schools (at least in terms of science and mathematics) to exert pressures for change, and reforms were made. The push, though, came from outside the educational system itself.

For international education to deal with a study of the world as a system, it seems likely that the thrust here must also come from outside. Unfortunately, though, organizations and individuals who might provide this push persist in looking at world problems through a nationalist lens, frequently in the mistaken belief that they are thus achieving a global view. The pressure for change within the educational system may not come unless these groups can transcend their present approach.

In other words, the long-range solutions might become possible if concerned organizations and societies could change the climate of opinion by beginning to explore

[2] Taylor, Harold, *The World and the American Teacher*, Washington, D.C., American Association of Colleges for Teacher Education, 1967, p. 26.

practical alternatives for solving our problems—alternatives that are cross-national, or international, or global. As was suggested earlier, this does not necessitate a major shift in philosophy. For example, in trying to define what constituted a "world corporation," Judd Polk ended up with this Cartesian approach:

> A company thinks world-wide, therefore it is a world company. It sees the world as one market and mobilizes its resources—capital, management, technology—to optimize its position everywhere.

> Judd Polk, "The Rise of World Corporations," *Saturday Review*, Nov. 22, 1969, p. 32.

The same practical approach could be developed by the dozens of organizations that are concerned with problems of population, race, ecology, poverty, urbanization, and conflict resolution. These groups must recognize what Lee Anderson has called ". . . the internationalization of many aspects of man's ageless problems of survival." [3] If such recognition can be developed in areas other than business, the impact will be felt in the educational world, too.

The hope provided by the view from the moon, then, is that it can help us to achieve, in Kelman's words, a "restructuring of reality"—the ability to see beyond the nation-state without destroying the nation-state. In a recent speech, James Becker stated: "To see the world as one is a necessary starting point and goal of international education. Such a view will not solve all of man's problems, but it may provide the vision and insight needed if man is to survive." [4]

[3] Anderson, Lee, "An Examination of the Structures and Objectives of International Education," *Social Education*, XXXII, Nov., 1968, p. 641.

[4] Becker, James, Unpublished transcript of address to the Texas Education Agency, August, 1969.

While waiting for a more favorable climate of opinion, of course, the individual teacher should not be content with simply accepting the parochialism of the traditional curriculum. He should become aware of, and make use of, changes already in progress. And, with something of a Fabian approach, he can take advantage of whatever flexibility exists within the system to offer students some understanding of the world as a system and mankind as a single species. Part II of this book will outline recent developments that seem headed in the right direction, and Part III will explore some of the strategies that might be used to insert a global perspective into the existing curriculum.

BIBLIOGRAPHY

Bellack, Arno, *et al.*, *The Language of the Classroom* (N.Y., Teachers College Press, 1967).

Billington, Ray A., *et al.*, *The Historian's Contribution to Anglo-American Misunderstanding: Report of a Committee on National Bias in Anglo-American History Textbooks* (London, Hobbs, Dorman & Co., 1966).

Black, Hillel, *The Schoolbooks* (N.Y., Charles Merrill, 1967).

Cantril, Hadley, *Human Dimension; Experiences in Policy Research* (New Brunswick, Rutgers University Press, 1967).

Hunt, Maurice P. and Lawrence E. Metcalf, *High School Social Studies: Problems in Reflective Thinking and Social Understanding* (N.Y., Harper, 1955).

Massialas, Byron and Benjamin Cox (eds.), *Social Studies*

in the United States (N.Y., Harcourt, Brace & World, 1967).

Oliver, Donald W. and James P. Shaver, *Teaching Public Issues in the High School* (Boston, Houghton-Mifflin, 1966).

Shaver, James P., "Reflective Thinking, Values, and Social Studies Textbooks," *The School Review*, 73, Autumn, 1965, p. 226.

PART II

STEPS IN THE RIGHT DIRECTION

Although the obstacles discussed in the previous chapter often seem insurmountable, there are some changes taking place in social studies education, with the promise of more to come. An increasing number of individual teachers and local school districts are engaged in a conscientious effort to make social studies courses relevant to the lives of their students. New methods of teaching are being developed, tested and, very gradually, disseminated. The major curriculum projects are breathing new life into at least a few of the dusty course offerings of the past, and a growing number of organizations are providing expertise and a wide variety of teaching tools.

1

The Curriculum
Projects

AFTER A NUMBER OF YEARS OF ACTIVITY, THE HOPE
engendered by the major curriculum projects still lies
more in the realm of potential than in change actually
accomplished. With some exceptions, textbook publishers have not yet shown the initiative displayed by
the projects themselves. Partly for this reason, the communications gap discussed earlier remains serious—the
innovations simply aren't getting into the classroom fast
enough.

Despite these qualifications, most participants in the
Study agreed that the projects could become a major
vehicle for change. The work of all of the projects was

reviewed, but limitations of time and space prevented a detailed survey of each. Instead, H. Thomas Collins presented a sample view of those projects whose material seemed most clearly related to the objectives of the Study.

Here, we will concentrate on two of the most important objectives developed by the Study: first, the study of man as a species; second, the study of the international system as *one* level of human social organization. A listing of the full titles and addresses of the projects mentioned is on pages 50–51.

Interdisciplinary Approaches to the Study of Man

A number of projects have developed material for the study of the development of man, including comparisons of man with other animals. At the elementary level, the Education Development Center has produced a variety of materials for *Man: A Course of Study,* designed for use in the upper elementary grades. The Anthropology Curriculum Project at the University of Georgia has developed a program to be used in grades one through six: *Concepts of Culture*—grades 1 and 4; *The Development of Man and His Culture*—grades 2 and 5; *Cultural Change*—grades 3 and 6.

For secondary grades, the Anthropology Curriculum Study Project[1] has prepared a sixteen-week unit (plus a smaller, condensed version) titled *Patterns in Human History.* With the help of an easily followed teacher's

---

[1] The *Anthropology Curriculum Study Project* is sponsored by the American Anthropological Association and is distinct from the *Anthropology Curriculum Project* at the University of Georgia.

guide, the course offers excellent tools for a social-science approach:

> Materials for the course are rich and varied, consisting of several sets of readings in paperback form, transparencies for the overhead projector, evidence cards, site maps, wall charts and photo displays, facsimiles of documents (e.g., translations of Sumerian tablets), casts of artifacts and fossils, filmstrips, and sound recordings. A substantial effort has been made by the Project staff to find ways of presenting data that are graphic but not too costly, that enable students to manipulate materials and make their own comparisons, that convey some sense of reality to what is otherwise a very abstract problem, that give students of diverse interests and abilities a chance to be productively involved in a genuine intellectual problem.
>
> Anthropology Curriculum Study Project, Newsletter, No. 8, Fall, 1969, p. 2.

All three of the projects mentioned include units on comparisons of man with other species, to show, in the words of Jerome Bruner, ". . . wherein man is distinctive in his adaptation to the world, and wherein there is discernible continuity between him and his animal forebearers." [2] These projects also illustrate the sort of cross-disciplinary approach that is needed in socal studies teaching.

In the area of understanding human similarities and differences, Collins found that there has been some progress, with an increasing number of schools offering (usually as electives) courses in psychology, sociology, and anthropology. There has been little effort, however, to insert information about human similarities into the

[2] Bruner, Jerome, Outline for *Man: A Course of Study*, Education Development Center, 1968.

standard texts for world history or world cultures. The books of Ethel Ewing (*Our Widening World*) and Leften Stavrianos (*A Global History of Man*) are major exceptions in providing students with some means of making comparisons among societies, but most texts tend to emphasize differences rather than similarities.

The study of human similarities and differences, of course, includes racial and cultural diversity, and a number of projects have produced materials on this topic. Here is a brief summary of those described in the Report:

1. The Minnesota Project has included, in its tenth grade U.S. History course, a long unit on the failure of social and economic rehabilitation of the Southern Negro in the years following the Civil War. The twelfth grade course (*Value Conflicts and Policy Decisions*) contains a unit on "resolving race problems."

2. The Indiana University Government Project, in its ninth grade course (*American Political Behavior*), treats the American Negro as one example of a political subculture. The unit examines ". . . the effects upon the total political socialization of an individual resulting from his being a member of a particular race. . . ." (p. 121)

3. The Harvard Project has produced a pamphlet titled *Negro Views of America: The Legacy of Oppression*, which uses social science methodology to explore such topics as how Negroes view our society.

4. The Carnegie-Mellon Project presents a comparative approach to race relations in two of the four units developed for the tenth grade course, *Tradition and Change in Four Societies*. Using an inquiry approach, the students gain some ideas of how race relations in this country are unique and ways in which they are similar to other multiracial societies. In addition, three chapters designed for the eleventh grade U.S. History course deal with the past

of the American Negro and his current struggle for equal rights.

The Study of International Society

The Study found that there was a good deal of material available on the study of sub-national groups. Curriculum planners and textbook publishers have given evidence of their conviction that the study of families, tribes, and cities is necessary for the understanding of human social organization. But, as Collins points out, the teacher who uses such material should make clear "the relationship between these groups and the larger societies of which they are a part." (p. 123)

In regard to teaching about national groups, it is probably safe to say that practically all students in the elementary grades are exposed to some information about other countries and areas of the world. However, as we stated earlier, there are weaknesses to this approach, which Collins sums up this way:

> Very often these efforts to study other countries or areas fall victim to the common practice of trying to cover too broad a sweep in too short a period of time. This has necessitated superficiality and undue emphasis upon the bizarre and the unique. Therefore, many elementary students have been left believing that all Norwegians are fishermen who live in a tiny village at the head of a fjord, or that all Greeks are villagers who daily go forth to extract sponges from the clear blue waters of the sea. (p. 123)

Much the same criticism can be applied to materials for use in high schools. At both levels, though, some of the projects have made attempts to give students a more realistic understanding of other countries and areas. The sort of efforts being made can be illustrated by the materials various projects have developed for teaching about Africa:

1. The Minnesota Project has created a two-year elementary sequence for the comparative study of *Families Around the World*. The teacher's guide states that "children will study families from different societies, including a family from a non-Western culture at each grade level. They will be asked to make comparisons with their own families. At the end of the year . . . (they) will be asked to generalize about families in their own communities as well as around the world."[3] The second grade unit on "the Hausa Family" stresses similarities with Western family structure as well as differences.

2. The Taba Project materials include a *Study of Comparative Communities*, and here, too, when elementary school children learn about communities in Africa, they are encouraged to make comparisons as well as contrasts. The use of what Dr. Taba called "large central ideas" provides the student with a set of generalizations that can help him to understand other communities in relation to his own.

3. The Providence Project has devoted the entire sixth grade course to an intensive comparison of Africa and Latin America. As with the Minnesota and Taba materials, a number of disciplines are included, but here the emphasis is on history and geography.

4. At the secondary level, the Harvard Project has recently published materials on *Colonial Kenya: Cultures in Conflict*. Historical and contemporary readings concentrate on "fundamental differences in the way Europeans and Kenyans view reality." This material, incidentally,

[3] Teacher's Guide to *Families Around the World*, Project Social Studies Center, University of Minnesota, p. 1.

illustrates ". . . the increasing willingness of several of the projects to deal in depth with current, often, open-ended, questions that require the students to make value judgments." (p. 126)

As mentioned in regard to race, the Carnegie-Mellon materials encourage students to see comparisons and contrasts between multi-racial societies in Africa, Latin America and the United States. Project Africa, which is now located at Carnegie-Mellon University, has produced a variety of materials for the study of sub-Saharan Africa, some for use in seventh through ninth grade courses in world geography or world cultures, and a one-semester twelfth grade course. "The major focus in these materials is on people, contemporary culture, and individual and group problems relevant to life in the latter part of the twentieth century." [4]

Very little material was found to be available on multi-national subjects. According to Collins: "A brief look at the United Nations, or perhaps a passing mention of the North Atlantic Treaty Organization, the Organization of American States or the European Common Market is often the total exposure to the rapidly growing area of cross-national groupings that students now receive in social studies courses." (p. 128)

Collins also points out the areas in which there has been little or no attempt to develop curriculum materials.

> The projects have largely chosen to avoid consideration of such topics as: the impact of corporations on global society, the mounting problems associated with population increases, the increased need for conflict resolution on both domestic and international levels, the pressing need to establish world-wide control of pollu-

[4] "A Summary of Project Activities," Project Africa, Carnegie-Mellon University, Pittsburgh, 1967, p. 1.

tion, the ever-widening gap between the "haves" and the "have-nots" of our world, the desirability of having available some form of supra-national order or control to assure peace, the whole complex area of foreign policy decision-making, the growing role of regional organizations and common markets. (p. 129)

In addition to these curriculum needs, it was felt that there should be developed an annotative bibliography or inventory of available resources, and something in the way of instruments for curriculum evaluation and planning guides that would allow school systems to self-evaluate and revise their curricula.

Although not discussed in this part of the Study, mention should be made here of the major efforts made by some state departments of education to revise the entire K-12 program. The following analysis is excerpted from a speech by James Becker:

> In addition to the experimental projects dealing with various segments of the social studies, several large-scale attempts have been made to deal with K-12 programs on a concept-development basis, that is, to identify major concepts, ideas and generalizations that might serve to structure the social studies throughout the student's school experience.
>
> The concept-development approach to organizing social studies instruction attempts to find ways of subsuming large quantities of factual material under a relatively small number of generalizations. This procedure will, it is hoped, drastically reduce the number of isolated facts to be remembered and center attention on guiding principles which students master by selecting and organizing the supporting factual evidence. It is not intended that basic concepts be presented as items to be memorized, but rather as analytical generalizations in illuminating ideas that will emerge from what has been studied. Students need to develop the concept

so that it *works for them;* memorizing a list of concepts is useless.

A number of states have produced social studies guidelines based on the principle of concept-development. In California more than two hundred social scientists worked with the State Central Committee on Social Studies to identify major concepts in the fields of anthropology, history, philosophy, sociology, psychology, geography, political science and economics. The result of their efforts is a guideline, soon to be released, entitled "California Statewide Social Sciences Study Committee: Preliminary K-12 Social Sciences Framework." Emphasizing modes of inquiry rather than particular data, the study asserts, "Pure content is of limited use. Development of attitudes and visceral understanding of how other people see themselves and the world around them should be our goal."

A state committee in Wisconsin followed a somewhat similar procedure in preparing a list of basic concepts and ideas drawn from each of the social science disciplines. Further examples of work by states include units on World Cultures prepared by Colorado and Pennsylvania, and a World Areas program developed by New York.

James Becker, Unpublished transcript of address to the Education Agency, August, 1969.

BIBLIOGRAPHY

Parker, Franklin, "Teaching International Understanding in High School: A Bibliographical Essay," *Phi Delta Kappan,* XLIX, Dec., 1967, p. 221.

"Teaching World Affairs Tomorrow," *Intercom,* 9, Sept.-Oct. 1967, N.Y., Foreign Policy Association.

Pennsylvania Department of Education, *Directory of So-*

cial Studies Curriculum Projects, Bureau of General & Academic Education, Box 911, Harrisburg, Pa., 1969.

Marin Social Studies Project, *Directory of Curriculum Projects,* 201 Tamal Vista Blvd., Corte Madera, Calif., 1969.

CURRICULUM PROJECTS DESCRIBED IN CHAPTER I

Anthropology Curriculum Project
University of Georgia
126 Fain Hall
Athens, Georgia 30601
Dr. Marion J. Rice
Dr. Wilfred C. Bailey

Anthropology Curriculum Study Project
5632 South Kimbark Avenue
Chicago, Illinois 60637
Dr. Malcolm Collier

Education Development Center, Inc.
Social Studies Curriculum Program
15 Mifflin Place
Cambridge, Mass. 02138
Dr. Peter B. Dow

A Geo-Historical Structure For Social
    Studies Curriculum Project
Rhode Island College
Providence, Rhode Island 02908
Dr. Ridgway F. Shinn, Jr.

Harvard Social Studies Project
Graduate School of Education
Harvard University
Cambridge, Mass. 02138
Dr. Don W. Oliver
Dr. Fred M. Newmann

Minnesota Social Studies Curriculum Project
College of Education
Department of Secondary Education
350A Peik Hall
University of Minnesota
Minneapolis, Minnesota 55455
Dr. Edith West

Project Africa
Baker Hall
Carnegie-Mellon University
Pittsburgh, Pennsylvania 15213
Dr. Barry K. Beyer

Social Studies Curriculum Development Center
Carnegie-Mellon University
Schenley Park
Pittsburgh, Pennsylvania 15213
Dr. Edwin Fenton

Social Studies Development Center
  (Government)
Indiana University
1129 Atwater Street
Bloomington, Indiana 47401
Dr. Howard Mehlinger

Taba Curriculum Development Project
Education Building, Room 10
San Francisco State College
San Francisco, California 94132
Dr. Norman E. Wallen

2

Innovations in
Teaching Methods

IN A POSITION PAPER PREPARED FOR THE STUDY, BRUCE
Joyce of Teachers College at Columbia University argued
that the teaching methods of the "new social studies" are
not likely to be widely used simply because teachers can't
use them. Here is the argument he presents:

> In any area which involves social values . . . there is
> quick agreement that no one wants to brainwash the
> young—to hand him a ready-made set of ideas and
> values. It is an easy step from that position to the
> recommendation that instruction should be carried on
> inductively. 'We'll show the kids the world perspective,'
> the argument goes in our case, 'and then let them form

their own ideas.' Thus reduced, one proceeds to develop inductive teaching strategies and back-up materials. So far, so good.

Then the trouble begins. One is rudely reminded that the teaching styles of most teachers do not adapt well to inductive teaching procedures. Whether one looks at teaching from the stance of Bellack,[1] Flanders,[2] Medley and Mitzel,[3] Hunt and Joyce,[4] or anyone else who has studied teaching with contemporary research tools, the answer has been the same. *Most* teachers work with directive, recitative or lecture styles, and these styles are persistent and difficult to change. Only the application of the most advanced training methods has any effect, and that often for only a small percentage of the teachers . . . A curriculum reform, then, which depends entirely on inductive teaching will almost surely fail. A reform that is accompanied by very powerful teacher training can use limited inductive strategies for some purposes. (p. 336)

One is forced to admit that Joyce's pessimism is realistic, and can be applied to almost any teaching innovation that strays from the traditional recitative style. And yet the hope persists that there are many teachers who would be willing to try some of the new social studies methods if they understood the rationale for them and how they would operate in the classroom. Again we are faced with a breakdown in communication. The majority of social studies teachers in this country are not fa-

[1] Bellack, Arno, *et al.*, *The Language of the Classroom* (N.Y., Teachers College Press, 1967).

[2] Flanders, Ned A., *Teacher Influence, Pupil Attitude, and Achievement* (Minneapolis, University of Minnesota Press, 1960).

[3] Medley, Donald M., and Mitzel, Howard E., "A Technique For Measuring Classroom Behavior," *Journal of Educational Psychology*, 1958, LXIX, 238–246.

[4] Hunt, David E., and Joyce, Bruce R., "Teacher Trainee Personality and Initial Teaching Style," *American Education Research Journal*, May, 1967, 4, 253–261.

miliar with the classroom approaches devised within the past few years.

This information gap presents a serious dilemma because, as the Study makes clear, one of our major needs is to stop teaching information and start teaching information-processing; the new social studies provide the tools for that transformation. As McClelland stated, ". . . The task of education in broadening, sharpening and disciplining the student's 'map of the social world' becomes largely that of developing skills and insights in information selection and processing." (p. 364)

One of the goals of the Study—and of the new social studies—is the creation of new roles for both students and teachers. The student should no longer be considered merely a receptacle in which the teacher deposits the information he himself acquired in similar fashion. Instead, the teacher helps the student develop skills and concepts which can guide him in his efforts to make sense out of data.

Perhaps a good way to illustrate this approach to learning is by using a hypothetical classroom dialogue described by McClelland. Although this little scenario is based on the use of a computer in a junior-high school classroom, it is a clear indication of the role changes talked about.

> STUDENT: "Do you think the Russians are better than the Chinese?"
> TEACHER: "In what way? What do you mean when you ask, are they better?"
> STUDENT: "Well, do the Russians make more good things for the people—like cars, movies, refrigerators? Maybe Russians have more good things to eat?"
> TEACHER: "Make a list of what you think are 'good things.' Then you can ask the computer for information." (*The student compiles his list and the questions are fed to the computer.*)

COMPUTER: "The data requested are as follows: . . ."

STUDENT: (*Studying the printout*): "See, the Russians are better."

TEACHER: "Yes, but you still didn't check to see how much better. You didn't think to find out how many people there are in each country, how much income they receive, which people get what you call the 'good things,' and whether or not China is making faster progress than Russia in producing the products on your list. Are you sure that being able to make and use things like cars would make the Russians better than the Chinese? But first you should get the additional information from the machine. You should write your questions so you can find out how much income the average person receives in both countries. Also, try to find out what the lowest 25 percent and the highest 25 percent receive. Do you know how to do that? Remember to convert to dollar equivalents."

STUDENT: "Yes."

COMPUTER: "The distribution of passenger motor vehicles in the U.S.S.R. is . . ., etc."

STUDENT: "I'll have the computer compare all this to the United States. Then I'm going to try to get information on two more things: Are Russians happier than the Chinese and do Russians have more freedom than the Chinese? When I do that, I am going to get the facts about happiness and freedom for the United States —and Sweden too—just to make it more interesting."

TEACHER: "You can't think of any way to show happiness, can you? You can think about that while you finish the comparison for the United States on population, income per capita, and the like."

STUDENT: "I already know some things to try for happiness. I'll use suicides, vacations people take, number of people in hospitals, murders, divorces, orphans, how long people live on the average, and maybe public opinion polls on what people say they worry about in all four countries. And, for freedom, I can check on elections, voters, churches, newspapers, and things like that."

TEACHER: "That's good but you probably will have

some problems. Just think about your indicators. You will have to convince me that they really stand for the things you say they stand for."

COMPUTER: "The requested data are not available as follows: . . ."

STUDENT: "I can't get data for vacations, churches, and polls for the People's Republic of China. There are some funny things too in the happiness index for Sweden and the U.S.S.R. I think Swedes are happier than the Russians, but the picture is mixed up. What do I do now?"

TEACHER: "Which are you going to believe—your personal impressions or your findings? You should know by now that interpreting your printouts is the hard part. There are validity problems with all sets of indicators; and in high school you will learn how to estimate the probable amount of error in your aggregated data and some ways to correct for it. Do the best you can with what you have now. What are you going to do about the missing data? You didn't get anything on Chinese vacations. How is that to be explained?"

STUDENT: "Our computer just doesn't know that. Or maybe they don't have vacations. Or maybe their government doesn't let out the information? That would be good for the freedom index—if I could find out what information is censored by the government. I guess the Chinese don't have vacations. I'll just drop vacations."

TEACHER: "It is possible that there are some data estimates on religion in China. If you want to follow that, I'll approve a question to the central network."

STUDENT: "I'll fill out the form."

(Later)

STUDENT: "I have everything completed now and it shows how Russia is better than China. But I don't think I can really decide. Anyway, the program turned out another way when I added the U.S. and Sweden."

TEACHER: "Go ahead and write your summary. Keep to the facts that you actually used and don't add a lot of statements about matters that you did not investigate. Show your conclusions but indicate which ones you

are sure about and which ones are less reliable, no matter how much you like them. Your choice of the original
question was a poor one, but I let you go ahead to see
if you could correct it; and you did quite well. Next
time you program, see if you can't make a series of more
precise and interesting comparisons. Maybe you could
follow up on David Smith's investigation of laws in five
countries which restrict individual freedom. Since you
started on freedom, you might want to look into it more
fully. You could analyze freedom of speech and press
for, perhaps, ten countries in the Atlantic area and see
what generalizations about legal restrictions can be
made for the period 1900 to the present. I think the
computer will provide you with all the information you
need."

Although the use of the computer simplifies this illustration, it does create an impressionistic picture of replac-
ing the "coverage" of subject matter with the sort of
inquiry approach that "creates relational, relevant knowledge." The use of the new social studies, of course, is not
without problems of its own. Joyce points out, for example, that we have not yet established a structure or
method of inquiry in international education, and much
of what we deal with in that area has a high emotional
content which might make teachers uncomfortable.

With the understanding that the innovations of the new
social studies are not likely to solve all our problems, they
nevertheless offer a giant step in the direction of more
relevant and more exciting learning. For most teachers,
the use of these methods requires a drastic retraining program. Although seeing the methods in operation is the
best way to find out about them, there is a good deal of
self-learning that can be done. For teachers and curriculum planners who are interested in embarking on such a
venture, we offer the following bibliographical essay by

G. Sidney Lester, Director of the Marin County Social Studies Project, Corte Madera, California.

The New Social Studies:
A Selected Bibliography and Review

Everybody talks about the new social studies, but nobody tells the classroom teacher what he can do about it. There have been some 70 or 80 social studies curriculum development projects at work during the past decade, but most have not yet produced many products for the classroom. Few school districts have purchased any of these new materials and only a handful of teachers have had the opportunity to use those. Add to this the fact that no one of these projects can be equated with "the new social studies" and the teacher in this field is presented with a very frustrating situation.

There are, however, two things the teacher can do to update his teaching. One is to get thoroughly retrained; the other is to read the right books. Probably the only sure method is to do both. In any case, once a teacher embarks on this path, he is likely to go through a period of educational culture shock. The reason for this is that he will soon become aware that the traditional social studies program is about 50 years out of date (based on a 1916 NEA Social Studies Commission report). No substantial changes have been made in this field until the past five or six years. We are currently teaching the wrong courses, in the wrong sequence, with the wrong, or no, psychological rationale. We have not kept up with the knowledge explosion, the advancements in the behavioral sciences or in today's social problems.

What kinds of changes will the teacher find in the books on the new social studies? First, he will find significant changes related to *teaching methods*. The new teaching methods do not deal with the mind as a receptacle for knowledge, but rather as a processor of data. The change, therefore, is not focused only on teaching methods, but also on learning processes.

Since new teaching methods must be compatible with

new learning processes, there is also a concern for the *structure* of the disciplines. This structure deals with data collection, concept formation, building generalizations, and the investigative processes used in scholarly research.

Another concern in the field has to do with updating content and subject matter. This not only implies including all of the social sciences, but emphasizing the *behavioral sciences* in the social studies program. A concern also is that history, geography, and government (civics) be taught so that students learn current trends in those fields. Those subjects usually are out of date as they are now taught.

Materials relating to the new social studies have come out so rapidly in the last five years it has been almost impossible to keep up with them or to know which ones are of greatest value. Here, then, is a recommended bibliography which will help redirect your thinking about teaching social studies:

Read Mager on objectives first. This very brief programmed text will help you find out what objectives are and how they should be stated. Unless objectives are stated specifically, we can't really know what to teach, let alone find out what students have learned.

Secondly, read Hunt and Metcalf. This text, although written in 1956 (recently revised), was the only "methods" book which contained any methods until 1965. This book provides a sound rationale for the reflective method and will also revise your thinking about what content is in the social studies (the "closed areas").

Next comes the inductive method. Fenton's first book best describes this, but you must play the game the book asks you to in order to experience the "ahas." Attempt to observe someone teaching inductively as you read this one. Induction and inquiry are not the same thing, but the distinction is difficult to understand. One anthology on this topic by Allen will help. A final, but unique, contribution in the methods area is what Oliver and Shaver call the jurisprudential method. Reading about these methods is not as useful as seeing them demonstrated, but teachers should be able to distinguish between them and also use them. When you focus on each of these methods, you should become a process-oriented teacher and will want to read why Parker and Rubin talk about "Process as Content."

The structure(s) of the social sciences is being rapidly incorporated into the social studies program, and it is necessary to understand both the parts and the whole of structure. Price's book provides a list of basic concepts, and a second publication from his project by Fancett deals with how to teach them. Womack tells how to teach generalizations inductively and explains the use and value of generalizations. Morrissett's book will explain structure, which shows the relationships between concepts and generalizations, and also explains dynamic systems used in the behavioral sciences. Three recent contributions to the literature dealing with structure are by Herbert, Lowe, and Feldman and Seifman.

One of our problems is that we have taught kids static, non-functional ways of looking at the world instead of ways that work. To sharpen your understanding of the impact of the social sciences, read Berelson and Steiner. The longer version is not only fascinating reading, but a must as a reference book in the classroom. Brodbeck and Bower and Hollister also describe the social sciences so that teachers can understand the nature of what it is we're trying to teach.

Somewhere along the line, it's necessary to become familiar with cognitive levels. Bloom is the most comprehensive text, but difficult to read. Sanders' book is based on Bloom and is more applicable to the classroom. A broader perspective on thinking will be found in the NCSS yearbook by Fair and Shaftel.

The companion to Bloom is Krathwohl's book on the affective domain. The whole area of attitudes, values, and affect is still pretty fuzzy, but Mager, Raths and Kiesler will provide some help. Shaftel and Shaftel, Boocock, and Nesbitt provide some practical ways of working in the affective area with role-playing and simulations.

Finally, Carr, Sowards, or Fenton's second book will

summarize where you have been or, if you prefer, read these first to get an overview of where you are going.

Advanced reading by social studies specialists, teacher trainers, or the well-informed department chairman should include some of the following: For rationale in social studies, try Shaver and Berlack, Brubaker's book on "Alternatives," or one by Kellum which you won't want to put down. Some advanced work on thinking and learning will be found in books by Gagne, Smith and Ennis, and Bruner. Materials on teacher effectiveness can be found in a basic text by Amidon and Flanders. Other systems are described in Simon and Boyer, and Biddle and Ellena.

Specifically for the elementary teacher, we should add the works of Clement, Jarolimek, Joyce, and Taba's handbook. More advanced material can be found in Brandwein and Herman.

If this seems like a long row to hoe, you're right. The list of good stuff seems endless, and yet this list is only a sampling. The teacher who is willing to start on this list is to be envied, because it will change his understanding of what it is to teach social studies and will improve his effectiveness dramatically. You will also find that teaching the new social studies is not dependent on the use of materials from one of the projects. The teacher who understands what it's all about will always do a better job than one who doesn't, regardless of the materials available.

BIBLIOGRAPHY

Allen, Rodney F., John V. Fleckenstein, and Peter M. Lyon, *Inquiry in the Social Studies, Theory and Examples for Classroom Teachers* (Washington, D.C., National Council for the Social Studies, Readings 2, 1968).

Amidon, Edmund J. and Ned A. Flanders, *The Role of the Teacher in the Classroom* (Minnesota, Amidon and Associates, Inc., 1967).

Berelson, Bernard and Gary Steiner, *Human Behavior— An Inventory of Scientific Findings* (New York, Harcourt, Brace & World, 1965).

Berelson, Bernard and Gary Steiner, *Human Behavior: Shorter Edition* (New York, Harcourt, Brace & World, 1967).

Berg, Harry D. (ed.), *Evaluation in Social Studies* (Washington, D.C., 35th Yearbook of the National Council for the Social Studies, 1965).

Biddle, Bruce and William J. Ellena, *Contemporary Research on Teacher Effectiveness* (New York, Holt, Rinehart & Winston, 1964).

Bigge, Morris L. *Learning Theories for Teachers* (New York, Harper & Row, 1964).

Bloom, Benjamin S., *et al.*, *Taxonomy of Educational Objectives, The Classifications of Educational Goals, Handbook I: Cognitive Domain* (New York, David McKay & Co., 1956).

Boocock, Sarane, *Simulation Games in Learning* (Beverly Hills, California, Stage Publishing Co., 1968).

Bower, Eli M. and William G. Hollister (eds.), *Behavioral Science Frontiers in Education* (New York, John Wiley & Sons, Inc., 1967).

Brandwein, Paul F., *Toward a Discipline of Responsible Consent, Elements in a Strategy for Teaching Social Sciences in the Elementary School* (New York, Harcourt, Brace & World, Inc., 1969).

Brodbeck, May (ed.), *Readings in the Philosophy of the Social Sciences* (New York, Macmillan Co., 1968).

Brubaker, Dale L., *Alternative Directions for the Social Studies* (Scranton, Pa.: International Textbook Co., 1967).
Brubaker, Dale L. (ed.), *Innovation in the Social Studies:*

Teachers Speak for Themselves (New York, Thomas Y. Crowell Co., 1968).

Bruner, Jerome S., Jacqueline J. Goodnow, and George A. Austin, *A Study of Thinking* (New York, John Wiley & Sons, 1967).

Carr, Edwin R., *The Social Studies* (New York, The Library of Education, Center for Applied Research in Education, Inc., 1966).

Clements, H. Millard, William R. Fielder, and B. Robert Tabachnick, *Social Study: Inquiry in Elementary Classrooms* (New York, Bobbs-Merrill Co., 1966).

Cox, Benjamin and Byron G. Massialas, *Social Studies in the United States, A Critical Appraisal* (New York, Harcourt, Brace & World, 1967).

Estvan, Frank J., *Social Studies in a Changing World, Curiculum and Instruction* (New York, Harcourt, Brace & World, Inc., 1968).

Fair, Jean and Fannie R. Shaftel (eds.), *Effective Thinking in the Social Studies* (Washington, D.C., 37th Yearbook of the National Council for the Social Studies, 1967).

Fancett, Verna C., *et al.*, *Social Science Concepts and the Classroom* (Syracuse, N.Y., Syracuse Univ., Social Studies Curriculum Center, 1968).

Feldman, Martin and Eli Seifman, *The Social Studies, Structure, Models, and Strategies* (Englewood Cliffs, N.J., Prentice-Hall, Inc., 1969).

Fenton, Edwin, *The New Social Studies* (New York, Holt, Rinehart & Winston, Inc., 1967).

Fenton, Edwin, *Teaching the New Social Studies in Secondary Schools—An Inductive Approach* (New York, Holt, Rinehart & Winston, 1966).

Fox, Robert, Margaret B. Luszki, and Richard Schmuck, *Diagnosing Classroom Learning* (Chicago, Science Research Associates, Inc., 1966).

Faser, Dorothy M. (ed.), *Social Studies Curriculum De-*

velopment (Washington, D.C., 39th Yearbook of the National Council for the Social Studies, 1969).

Gagne, Robert M., *The Conditions of Learning* (New York, Holt, Rinehart & Winston, Inc., 1965).

Goldmark, Bernice, *Social Studies, A Method of Inquiry* (Belmont Calif., Wadsworth Publishers, 1968).

Gross, Richard E., Walter McPhie, and Jack R. Fraenkel, *Teaching the Social Studies, What, Why and How* (Scranton, Pa., International Textbook Co., 1969).

Hebert, Louis J. and William Murphy (eds.), *Structure in the Social Studies* (Washington, D.C., National Council for the Social Studies, Readings 3, 1968).

Herman, Wayne L., *Current Research in Elementary School Social Studies* (Toronto, The Macmillan Co., 1969).

Hess, Robert D. and Judith V. Torney, *The Development of Political Attitudes in Children* (New York, Anchor, Doubleday and Co., 1968).

Hunt, Maurice P. and Lawrence E. Metcalf, *Teaching High School Social Studies* (New York, Harper & Row, 1968).

Jarolimek, John, *Social Studies in Elementary Education*, 3d ed. (New York, The Macmillan Co., 1965).

Jarolimek, John and Huber M. Walsh, *Readings for Social Studies in Elementary School* (New York, The Macmillan Co., 1967).

Joyce, Bruce R., *Strategies for Elementary Social Science Education* (Chicago, Science Research Associates, 1965).

Kellum, David F., *The Social Studies, Myths and Realities* (New York, Sheed & Ward, 1969).

Kiesler, Charles A., Barry S. Collins, and Norman Miller, *Attitude Change, A Critical Analysis of Theoretical Approaches* (New York, John Wiley & Sons, Inc., 1969).

Krathwohl, David R., *et al.*, *Taxonomy of Educational Objectives, The Classification of Educational Goals, Handbook II: Affective Domain* (New York, David McKay & Co., 1964).

Lowe, William T., *Structure and the Social Studies* (Ithaca, N.Y., Cornell University, 1969).

Mager, Robert F., *Developing Attitudes Toward Learning* (Palo Alto, Fearon Publishers, 1968).

Mager, Robert F., *Preparing Instructional Objectives* (San Francisco, Fearon Publishers, 1962).

Massialas, Byron G. and C. Benjamin Cox, *Inquiry in the Social Studies* (New York, McGraw-Hill, Inc., 1966).

Massialas, Byron G. and Andreas M. Kazamias, *Crucial Issues in the Social Studies* (Englewood Cliffs, N. J., Prentice-Hall, Inc., 1964).

Massialas, Byron G. and Frederick R. Smith, *New Challenges in the Social Studies* (Belmont, Calif., Wadsworth Publishing Co., 1965).

Massialas, Byron G. and Jack Zevin, *Creative Encounters in the Classroom: Teaching and Learning Through Discovery* (New York, John Wiley & Sons, 1967).

McLendon, Jonathan C., *Readings on Social Studies in Secondary Education* (New York, The Macmillan Co., 1966).

Michaelis, John U., *Social Studies for Children in a Democracy: Recent Trends and Developments*, 3d ed. (Englewood Cliffs, N.J., Prentice-Hall, 1963).

Michaelis, John U. and A. Montgomery Johnston, *The Social Sciences—Foundations of the Social Studies* (Boston, Allyn & Bacon, 1965).

Morrissett, Irving (ed.), *Concepts and Structure in the New Social Science* (New York, Holt, Rinehart & Winston, Inc., 1967).

Muessig, Raymond H. and Vincent R. Rogers, *Social Science Seminar Series*, 6 vols. (Columbus, Charles E. Merrill Books, 1965).

The Study of Anthropology. Peretti J. Pelto

Political Science: An Informal Overview. Francis J. Sorauf

Sociology: The Study of Man in Society. Caroline B. Rose

The Nature and Study of History. Henry Steele Commager

Economics and Its Significance. R. S. Martin and R. G. Miller

Geography: Its Scope and Spirit. Jan O. M. Broek

Nesbitt, William A. (ed.), *Simulation Games* (New York, Thomas Y. Crowell Co., 1970).

Oliver, Donald W. and James P. Shaver, *Teaching Public Issues in High School* (Boston, Houghton Mifflin Co., 1966).

Parker, J. Cecil and Louis J. Rubin, *Process as Content: Curriculum Design and the Application of Knowledge* (Chicago, Rand McNally and Co., 1966).

Patrick, John J., *Political Socialization of American Youth: Implications for Secondary School Social Studies,* Research Bulletin 3 (Washington, D.C., National Council for the Social Studies, 1967).

Price, Roy A., *et al., Major Concepts for the Social Studies* (Syracuse, N.Y., Syracuse University, Social Studies Curriculum Center, 1965).

Raths, Louis E., Merrill Harmin, and Sidney B. Simon, *Values and Teaching* (New York, Charles E. Merrill, 1966).

Raths, Louis J., *et al., Teaching for Thinking* (New York, Charles E. Merrill, 1967).

Rubin, Louis J. (ed.), *Life Skills in School and Society* (Washington, D.C., ASCD Yearbook, 1969).

Sanders, Norris M., *Classroom Questions, What Kinds?* (New York, Harper & Row, 1966).

Shaftel, Fannie R. and George Shaftel, *Role Playing for*

the Social Studies (Englewood Cliffs, N.J., Prentice-Hall, Inc., 1967).

Shaver, James R. and Harold Berlak, *Democracy, Pluralism and the Social Studies, Readings and Commentary, An Approach to Curriculum Decisions in the Social Studies* (Boston, Houghton Mifflin Co., 1968).

Simon, Anita and E. Gil Boyer, *Mirrors for Behavior, An Anthology of Classroom Observation Instruments* (Philadelphia, Research for Better Schools, Inc., 1967).

Smith, B. Othanel and Robert H. Ennis, *Language and Concepts in Education* (Chicago, Rand McNally and Co., 1969).

Smith, Fred R. and C. Benjamin Cox, *New Strategies and Curriculum in Social Studies* (Chicago, Rand McNally and Co., I969).

Smith, James A., *Creative Teaching of the Social Studies in the Elementary School* (New York, Allyn & Bacon, 1967).

Sowards, G. Wesley, *The Social Studies Curriculum Proposals for the Future* (Chicago, Scott Foresman & Co., 1963).

Taba, Hilda, *Teachers' Handbook for Elementary Social Studies* (Reading, Mass., Addison-Wesley Publishing Co., 1967).

Taba, Hilda, *Teaching Strategies and Cognitive Functioning in Elementary School Children* (San Francisco State College, USOE, 1966).

Womack, James G., *Discovering the Structure of the Social Studies* (New York, Benziger Bros., 1966).

3

Resources
for Teachers

THE PURPOSE OF THIS CHAPTER IS TO GIVE THE TEACHER OR
curriculum planner a brief reference guide to some of the
materials available in the field of social studies in general,
as well as more specifically in the area of international
education. The listings do not cover *all* of the sources that
might be of help; however, for each of the categories into
which the chapter is divided, we have tried to list the
major sources and also to suggest where more complete
listings may be found. Unfortunately, there is no way to
include the many simulations which have been designed
and produced by school systems.

Simulation Games

As far as school use is concerned, simulation games are of fairly recent origin. Since their first appearance about a decade ago, they have steadily increased in both popularity and sophistication. New games are now being designed, tested and published faster than we can keep track of them. The number of simulation games in the social studies alone now totals over one hundred.

Most teachers who have had experience with this teaching device have become convinced that simulations are a valuable addition to the arsenal of classroom aids, but no one has been able to determine precisely what their benefits are. Perhaps the most obvious advantage they offer is that they are great motivators. Something happens in a game. Everyone knows it's only a simulation of reality, but still they become very deeply involved in it—so deeply that they frequently seem to forget it's a game. Certain other advantages have emerged. In simulations of international affairs, for example, students seem to develop an understanding of—or a feeling for—the pressures placed on decision-makers. Simulation games have also proved effective in dramatizing many social problems, such as racial tensions and urban crises.

We still have much to learn before we can say exactly what simulations are good for and what their limitations are. Paul A. Twelker of Oregon State University outlines some of the areas we need to learn more about:

> While progress is being made in the application of simulation procedures to education, a host of problems still need to be resolved . . . We have no clear idea of the nature or range of application. We do not have available models of simulation design that might guide the developers as they specify what form and shape the

simulation is to take. We have little idea as to what type of simulation is most appropriate for the various types of learning. We have little information as to the effectiveness of simulation techniques as compared with some alternative training procedures in bringing about educational objectives.

Paul A. Twelker (ed.), *Instructional Simulation Systems; an Annotated Bibliography*, Continuing Education Publications, Corvallis, Oregon, 1969, p. 1.

A more complete discussion of the values, prospects and limitations of simulation games can be found in *Simulation Games*, by William Nesbitt (Thomas Y. Crowell Co., 1971). This book also contains a descriptive listing of games available, as well as a bibliography of pertinent books and articles.

Other major bibliographies are

1. Paul A. Twelker (ed.), *Instructional Simulation Systems; an Annotated Bibliography*, Continuing Education Publications, Corvallis, Oregon, 1969.

2. Macalester College Simulation Center, *Directory of Educational Simulations, Learning Games and Didactic Units* (Macalester College, Saint Paul, Minnesota 55101, 1969).

Producers of Simulations

Abt Associates, Inc.
55 Wheeler Street, Cambridge, Massachusetts 02138

Academic Games Director
Nova High School
3600 Southwest 70th Avenue, Fort Lauderdale, Florida 33314

Academic Games Project
Center for the Study of Social Organization of Schools

Student involvement in Simulation-Games
Photo Credit: Bernard Pierre Wolff

The Johns Hopkins University
3505 North Charles Street, Baltimore, Maryland 21212

Didactic Systems, Inc.
Post Office Box 500, Westbury, Long Island, New York 11590

Education Development Center, Inc.
15 Mifflin Place, Cambridge, Massachusetts 02138

Envirometrics
Science Resources Corporation
1100 17th Street, N.W., Washington, D.C. 20036

Foreign Policy Association School Services
345 East 46th Street, New York, N.Y. 10017

High School Geography Project
Post Office Box 1095, Boulder, Colorado 80302

Instructional Simulations, Inc.
2147 University Avenue, St. Paul, Minnesota 55114

Interact
Post Office Box 262, Lakeside, California 92040

International Academic Games
440 Las Olas Boulevard, Fort Lauderdale, Florida 33301

Joint Council on Economic Education (Bibliography)
1212 Avenue of the Americas, New York, N. Y. 10036

Science Research Associates
259 East Erie Street
Chicago, Illinois 60611

Teaching Research
A Division of the Oregon State System of Higher Education
Monmouth, Oregon 97361

Western Behavioral Sciences Institute
1121 Torrey Pines Boulevard, La Jolla, California 92037

Western Publishing Company, Inc.
School and Library Department
850 Third Avenue, New York, N.Y. 10022

Resource Organizations in World Affairs

The following list of organizations can provide teachers
and curriculum planners with assistance in a variety of
ways. Their range of activities includes curriculum materials, publications, newsletters, audio-visual aids, research
assistance and consultation, speakers, and teachers'
guides. The listing does not imply endorsement by the
author or the publisher.

ORGANIZATION	ACTIVITIES
African American Institute 866 United Nations Plaza New York, N.Y. 10017	Materials center, school services program, teacher's kits and guides, bibliographies, newsletter.
American Association of Colleges for Teacher Education 1201 Sixteenth Street, N.W. Washington, D.C., 20036	Publications; consultation on teacher education.
American Association of School Administrators— Association for the Advancement of International Education 1201 Sixteenth Street, N.W. Washington, D.C. 20036	Consultation; publications.
American Council on Education Commission on	Materials; publishes *Educational Record, Higher Education and National*

International Education
1785 Massachusetts Avenue
Washington, D.C. 20036

Affairs; Bulletin on International Education.

American Friends Service
Committee
160 N. 15th Street
Philadelphia, Pa. 19102

Seminars, conferences, materials, films, speakers.

American Political Science
Association
1527 New Hampshire Avenue, N.W.
Washington, D.C. 20036

Sponsors social studies project for elementary and secondary teachers; publishes newsletter and *American Political Science Review.*

Asia Society
112 East 64th Street
New York, N.Y. 10021

Bibliographies; periodical: *Asia and Asian Art;* study guides; audio-visual material.

Association For Asian
Studies
48 Lane Hall
University of Michigan
Ann Arbor, Mich. 48104

Research materials; bibliographies; periodical: *Journal of Asian Studies,* newsletter.

Atlantic Council of the U.S.
1616 H Street, N.W.
Washington, D.C. 20006

Speakers bureau; program consultation; resource materials; periodicals: *Atlantic Community Quarterly, Atlantic Community News.*

Atlantic Information
Centre for Teachers
23–25 Abbey House
8 Victoria Street
London, SW 1 England

Publishes newsletter; background and position booklets.

Carnegie Endowment for

Research materials, period-

International Peace
345 East 46th Street
New York, N.Y. 10017

icals: *International Concil-
iation.*

Center for the Study of
Democratic Institutions
P.O. Box 4068
Santa Barbara, Calif. 93103

Conferences, publications
and research reports; pe-
riodical: *Center Magazine.*

Center for Teaching
International Relations
Graduate School of
International Studies
University of Denver
Denver, Colorado 80210

Publishes newsletter; holds
conferences and in-service
institutes; provides consultation.

Center for War/Peace
Studies
218 E. 18th Street
New York, N.Y. 10003

Program consultation;
clearinghouse for mate-
rials; periodicals: *War/
Peace Report; Intercom.*

Council on Foreign
Relations
58 East 68th Street
New York, N.Y. 10021

Conferences; research ma-
terials; periodical: *Foreign
Affairs.*

Council on International
Educational Exchange
777 United Nations Plaza
New York, N.Y. 10017

Clearinghouse for mate-
rials; publications.

Council on International
Relations and United
Nations Affairs (CIRUNA)
833 United Nations Plaza
New York, N.Y. 10017

Program consultation;
sponsors Model U.N.; pub-
lishes newsletter **and**
Program Notes.

Education and World
Affairs
522 Fifth Avenue
New York, N.Y. 10036

Newsletter: *International
Education;* reference and
program assistance.

Foreign Policy Association
345 East 46th Street
New York, N.Y. 10017

Program consultation; materials; conferences and seminars; sponsors "Great Decisions" program; newsletter; *Headline Series; Great Decisions.*

Institute for International
Education
809 United Nations Plaza
New York, N.Y. 10017

Materials clearinghouse; program and research consultation; issues materials and publications.

International Schools
Services
392 Fifth Avenue
New York, N.Y. 10018

Curriculum consultation; conferences.

International Studies
Association
University of Minnesota
Minneapolis, Minnesota
55455

Professional association for international and comparative studies specialists. Section on teaching international relations.

Japan Society
250 Park Avenue
New York, N.Y. 10017

Conferences and seminars; program consultation; speakers; publications; audio-visual aids.

Joint Council on Economic
Education
1212 Avenue of the
Americas
New York, N.Y. 10036

Publications; curriculum consultation; newsletter; bibliographies.

Middle East Institute
1761 N Street, N.W.
Washington, D.C. 20036

Conferences; materials; periodical: *Middle East Journal.*

National Association of
Secondary School
Principals

Publications; quarterly bulletin.

1201 Sixteenth Street, N.W.
Washington, D.C. 20036

National Committeee on U.S.-China Relations 777 United Nations Plaza New York, N.Y. 10017	Conferences; speakers; materials; periodical: *China Clearinghouse*.
National Council for the Social Studies 1201 Sixteenth Street, N.W. Washington, D.C. 20036	Research and surveys; periodical: *Social Education*.
National Education Association Committee on International Relations 1201 Sixteenth Street, N.W. Washington, D.C. 20036	Conducts NEA Teacher Corps; periodical: *Today's Education*.
National Peace Corps Tape Bank Leyden High Schools 3400 Rose Street Franklin Park, Ill. 60131	Audio-tapes relating experiences of Peace Corps returnees.
Organization of American States Association 19th Street & Constitution Ave., N.W. Washington, D.C. 20006	Program consultation; publications.
Planned Parenthood— World Population 515 Madison Avenue New York, N.Y. 10022	Conferences; curriculum consultation; films; speakers; publications.
Population Association of America P.O. Box 14182 Benjamin Franklin Station Washington, D.C. 20044	Conferences; bibliographies; newsletter; quarterly journal.

Population Council 245 Park Avenue New York, N.Y. 10017	Research materials.
Population Crisis Committee 1730 K Street, N.W. Washington, D.C. 20006	Speakers; materials; publishes *Population Crisis* (occasional).
Population Reference Bureau 1755 Massachusetts Avenue Washington, D.C. 20036	Issues research studies; periodical: *Population Bulletin.*
Society for Citizen Education in World Affairs 122 Social Science Building University of Minnesota Minneapolis, Minn. 55455	Newsletter.
Sociological Resources for Secondary Schools American Sociological Association 503 First National Building Ann Arbor, Mich. 48108	Materials; publications.
Twentieth Century Fund 41 East 70th Street New York, N.Y. 10021	Publishes studies; audiovisual aids; newsletter.
United Nations Association 833 United Nations Plaza New York, N.Y. 10017	Sponsors U.N. Day; local chapters; conferences; materials; speakers; periodical: *Vista*; newsletter.
United States Committee for UNICEF 331 East 38th Street New York, N.Y. 10016	Elementary school materials; filmstrips.

World Law Fund
11 West 42nd Street
New York, N.Y. 10036

Conferences and seminars; curriculum and audio-visual materials; newsletter; publications.

World Tapes For
Education
P.O. Box 15703
Dallas, Texas 75215

Promotes international audio tape exchange.

In addition to these sources, teachers can learn of other materials from local World Affairs Councils and a number of government agencies, such as the U.S. Office of Education (particularly the Institute of International Education), and the Government Printing Office, Washington, D.C. 20402.

Films and Television

In addition to the commercial firms that sell or rent films, a number of universities offer rental services to schools within their general geographic area. Three of the major film centers are

1. Syracuse University School of Education
   926 South Crouse St.,
   Syracuse, N.Y. 13210
2. Indiana University School of Education
   445 No. Pennsylvania St.,
   Indianapolis, Indiana 46204
3. University of California,
   Berkeley School of Education
   Berkeley, Calif. 94720

Although there is no general clearinghouse for available films, tapes, and television documentaries, many of

the resource organizations listed above can help you find
material related to their field of interest. In addition, some
educational periodicals contain regular features on new
audio-visual materials. Among these publications are

1. *Civic Leader*
   Civic Education Service, Inc.
   1733 K Street, N.W., Washington, D.C. 20006
2. *Social Education*
   National Council for the Social Studies
   1201 Sixteenth St., N.W., Washington, D.C. 20036
3. *Media & Methods*
   134 North 13th Street, Philadelphia, Pa. 19107

There is also a periodical devoted to educational uses
of television: *Educational Television,* 140 Main Street,
Ridgefield, Conn. 06877. And many local stations, as well
as some public libraries, issue releases of forthcoming programs that would be of interest to teachers. A long-range
schedule of planned programs is available in pamphlet
form from Teacher's Guide to Television, Inc., P.O. Box
564, Lenox Hill Station, New York, N.Y. 10021 ($1.00 per
semester, $2.00 per year).

PART III

SOME
STRATEGIES
FOR CHANGE

There is no acceptable way to construct a detailed curriculum for grades K through 12 and to put it into general practice. The large differences in student abilities and experience, the wide variations in educational philosophy and practice from district to district and region to region of the country, the disparities in educational expectations among teachers and administrators, the traditions of local autonomy, and the resistance to centralization and standardization all militate against the prevalence of any single plan. (p. 362)

The above quotation from McClelland's position paper makes it clear that the Study is calling for a variety of change strategies, rather than a single program of reform. In other words, the individual teacher should select those innovations that can work in his situation, and at least begin to move in the directions outlined by the Study. Although a thorough revamping of the curriculum would be ideal, there is much that can be done without altering the basic structure of courses now being offered. Anderson has stressed the point that current curricula contain much of the information that is needed for a global view, and that major improvements can be made if teachers learn to emphasize the global perspective and thus give students a cognitive framework into which they can fit the information they receive.

In this section, we will suggest a few of the ways in which the current curriculum can be internationalized without becoming involved in the ambitious—and frequently futile— task of trying to devise new courses. The final two chapters will offer illustrations of complete study units that can be inserted into existing courses.

A word of caution: even the modest changes outlined here are likely to be met with resistance by many teachers, primarily because they suggest acceptance of the view of education "as a process to change learned behavior." Educators who feel that their role is only to reinforce and accentuate prevailing attitudes will find little of interest in these suggestions. Mehlinger put the matter rather strongly:

> To conceive the social studies teacher's role in internationalizing the social studies curriculum as being primarily that of changing student attitudes and imposing cognitions not already part of the community culture is not the most certain path to win popular endorsement. But, that is the task. To do less than this is to continue to muck-around, mouthing pious cliches. (p. 373)

1

Internationalizing the Current Curriculum[1]

World History Course

ORGANIZING THE STANDARD WORLD HISTORY OR WORLD CUL-
tures course to present a global view is an excellent way
of helping students to grasp the uses and meanings of
history. Instead of the confusion of the chronological or
"civilization" breakdown, students will gain an understanding of the "global history of man," and they can

[1] Much of this chapter is based on a paper prepared for the Study
by Howard Mehlinger, titled "Building an International Component
into the High School Social Studies Curriculum," pp. 372–385.

then relate the story of individual groups to the larger picture. This is pretty much the rationale for a few innovative textbook offerings, notably those of McNeill [2] and Stavrianos.[3]

In reviewing such global approaches to world history, Mehlinger writes:

> While various attempts to build a global or planetary approach to the history of human experience may differ in detail, they begin with shared assumptions: that all men are members of the same species occupying the same essential physical location, planet earth. The history of man should reveal the history of the species, both the separate development of individual human groups and their interconnectedness. (pp. 375–76)

The broad outlines of the sort of organization Mehlinger envisages might look something like this:

The Development of Early Man

Instead of starting with one of the early civilizations, such as Egypt or Sumer, the course would ". . . begin by treating the process by which man became human." The class would study the contributions of archaeology and anthropology. "As the Anthropology Curriculum Study Project has demonstrated, the investigation of hypotheses about early man can provide an unusual opportunity to make clear to youngsters the essence of social science techniques and the nature of knowledge." (p. 376)

[2] McNeill, William H., *The Rise of the West: A History of the Human Community* (U. of Chicago Press, 1963).
[3] Stavrianos, Leften, *Global History of Man* (Allyn & Bacon, Inc., 1966).

The Agricultural Revolution

This would be studied as an event which occurred over a long span of time and in at least two or three different areas of the world. Students would learn how the change from hunting to farming affected society in a variety of ways, such as material culture, population size, religion, and patterns of settlement.

The Development of Cities, Trade, and Warfare

This portion of the course would explain the development of early civilizations and the processes of cultural diffusion.

The Early Civilizations

These would be studied, not as separate and distinct phenomena, but as *"examples* of a general process that developed and spread across much of the planet to the late eighteenth and early nineteenth centuries." The students would analyze the agricultural bases of these civilizations, and the processes by which they expanded until they dominated much of the globe by the time of the Industrial Revolution. Later, agricultural civilizations began to give way to industrial ones, but examples of earlier civilizations and the various stages they went through still exist in parts of the world today.

The idea is that such an approach will give students a framework that can help them to a better understanding of the modern world. In today's Africa, for example, one can see various stages of civilization, ranging from the hunting and gathering groups of the Pygmies and Bushmen, through a middle-range of societies similar to those first communities that depended upon agriculture, to the highly developed states of the extreme north and south. If the student sees a pattern to man's experience, he can fit these varied cultures into that pattern.

Mehlinger concludes by saying:

> The vague, generalized conception of planetary history contained in the paragraphs above will not satisfy many people. They will point out the many exceptions that can be made to each of the generalizations. They will suggest many ways in which specific human societies were and are unique. Indeed, in trying to present a planetary view of history, one must necessarily dilute the unique experience of separate regions of the world. But, if our purpose is to prepare students for a world in which they will live as adults, and if residents of the planet are becoming more, rather than less, interconnected, some dilution of unique experience may be worth the rewards to be gained when students begin to acquire global perceptions. (p. 378)

American History

For American history courses, Mehlinger suggests that students' views can be broadened by helping them to look at U.S. events from the perspective of other countries. An excellent resource book for this purpose is *How Others See Us*,[4] a collection of textbook accounts from 34 nations on different aspects of the American experience.

A single quotation, from a French selection on American culture, will suggest how this approach might contribute to new perceptions:

[4] This book was prepared by the International Textbook Project, co-sponsored by Phi Delta Kappa, the National Council for the Social Studies, and the Service Center for Teachers of History of the American Historical Association (Houghton Mifflin, 1969).

The ascension of the United States to first rank is accompanied by a progression of their influence in the hierarchy of values in civilization. They are taking a more and more active part in the building of western civilization of which they are now one of the centers. But this is not all. The current exchange between Europe and America has been reversed in several fields. While over a period of some centuries America looked to Europe for inspiration, for models, it often happens today that the initiative comes from beyond the Atlantic: for the cinema, the novel, the theatre, architecture, sociology, the humanities, or the natural sciences, the techniques of production or the arrangement of daily living, for 'style of life,' American civilization is in process of becoming a model the attraction of which does not cease to grow beyond the frontiers of the American Union . . . The eventuality that American civilization may become one day the universal civilization is not at all inconceivable.

Donald Robinson (ed.), *As Others See Us* (Houghton Mifflin Co., 1969).

Although not all the selections view the U.S. experience so favorably, there is some question about the effect of such quotes on the perceptions of American students. Mehlinger writes that such material "could further the 'I am the greatest' syndrome that marks the ethnocentric personality; on the other hand, it may open a student's eyes, enabling him to see the degree to which his nation and national culture have become part of the world experience." (p. 381)

The teacher can achieve similar results by using selected articles from *Atlas* magazine, or even some of the foreign newspapers, in English, that can be found in many public and university libraries.

Another way to graft a global perspective onto the standard U.S. history course is through the use of comparative studies. One of the titles in this *New Dimensions* series (*Teaching the Comparative Approach to American Studies,* Thomas Y. Crowell Co., 1971) provides guidelines for teachers in creating comparative units on such topics as revolution, nationalism, race relations, economic development, and interventionism. The rationale for such an approach should now be clear: if students see similarities between events in the United States and other areas of the world (in addition to points of uniqueness), they will develop a different perception of the American experience: at the same time, particular events in our history come into sharper focus when compared with similar events elsewhere.

One of the few history texts that attempts to place U.S. history in a comparative setting is the two-volume *History of a Free People* (Macmillan Co., 1970), by Bragdon, Cole and McCutchen. Mention should also be made of some of the materials produced in the Harvard AEP series; especially the booklets on *The American Revolution* (American Education Publications, 1967).

Civics and Elective Courses

The traditional ninth and twelfth grade civics courses, plus the variety of twelfth grade electives (such as the "problems" courses) offer excellent opportunities for the inquiry-comparative approaches urged by the Study. The civics courses, particularly, have usually been thought of as "citizenship" courses, designed to acquaint students with the structures and functions of American political institutions. These courses are frequently among the least popular in the whole curriculum, and the research of Patrick[5] and others has shown that "much of what is

[5] Patrick, John J., *Political Socialization of American Youth,* (Bloomington, Indiana, High School Curriculum Center in Government, Indiana University, 1967).

currently taught in (these) courses is already possessed by students prior to taking the course." (p. 382)

In the light of the concerns of the Study, Mehlinger pictures a new role for these subjects:

> It might be argued that an entirely new 'citizenship' course is required because an entirely new form of citizenship is beginning to appear. If one can begin to talk seriously about planetary citizenship, it may be that the civics courses that once served to inculcate the American political culture to foreign born can be reconstituted to prepare ethnocentric Americans for the responsibilities of planetary citizenship. (pp. 382–83)

There is already a good deal of material available for the high school level that would allow teachers to internationalize and modernize their civics, economics, and government courses. The Carnegie-Mellon project, for example, has divided the ninth grade course into two semester offerings, the first dealing with *Comparative Political Systems*, and the second with *Comparative Economic Systems*. Using an inquiry approach, these texts offer an extremely readable selection of accounts comparing the political and economic systems of the Soviet Union, the United States, and one "primitive" (nonmodern) culture. The study is conducted with the help of some basic analytical questions; e.g., "Who are the political leaders and how are they recruited? How are decisions made in the society? Who decides what goods will be produced, how goods will be produced, and for whom?" Mehlinger points out that, "Questions such as these are transferable to other political and economic systems, thereby preventing students from becoming culture-bound in political and economic investigations." (p. 383)

In a somewhat similar fashion, the Indiana University project's ninth grade course in *American Political Be-*

havior provides a set of social science concepts that can be applied to other societies. In the twelfth grade course (*American and Comparative Political Systems*), an analytical model is developed through the study of the American system and then applied to studies of the political systems of England, the Soviet Union, and one non-modern nation.

Much of what we have said about the global perspective quite obviously applies to those twelfth grade courses known by such titles as American problems or problems of democracy. By globalizing theapproach to such topics as conservation, urbanization, race relations and war-prevention, the teacher will be "adding to students' understanding of the nature of the problems while providing them a much broader perspective than they would gain otherwise." (p. 384)

Mehlinger offers this conclusion on the internationalizing of current course offerings:

> . . . It is not necessary to install entirely new courses in order to build international perspectives into the social studies curriculum. All that is needed is for teachers and curriculum developers to begin to understand what the notion of a planetary society means. They will find an adequate number of opportunities to plug relevant concepts into existing courses, and students will begin to acquire some of the perspectives they will need to function as citizens of a world society. (p. 385)

BIBLIOGRAPHY

Becker, James, and Howard Mehlinger (eds.), *International Dimensions in the Social Studies* (38th Yearbook of the National Council for the Social Studies, Washington, D.C., 1968).

Patrick, John J., *Political Socialization of American Youth* (Bloomington, Indiana, High School Curriculum Center in Government, Indiana University, 1967).

Rogers, Vincent R., "Ethnocentrism in the Social Studies," *Phi Delta Kappan*, XLIX, Dec., 1967, p. 209.

Stavrianos, Leften, "A Global Perspective in the Organization of World History," in *New Perspectives in World History* (34th Yearbook of the National Council for the Social Studies, Washington, D.C., 1964).

Taylor, Harold, *The World and the American Teacher* (Washington, D.C. American Association of Colleges for Teacher Education, 1967).

Woodward, C. Vann (ed.), *The Comparative Approach to American History* (New York, Basic Books, Inc., 1968).

2

A Global Unit
for Secondary Schools

WITH A REASONABLE AMOUNT OF PREPARATION, TEACHERS
can develop units on a wide variety of topics that will
help students gain the sort of global perspective we have
been discussing. Race relations, ecology, and population
are among the subjects that have been mentioned earlier.
The sample unit mentioned here is based on the multinational corporation.

Although economic units are notoriously unpopular
with social studies teachers, you will find that this particular topic is not only important, but also exciting and surprisingly easy to teach. Here are some of the reasons for
this choice.

The Rationale

In the first place, paraphrasing the credo of mountain-climbers, we ought to teach it because it's there. Not only is the multinational corporation a fact of global living, but it's one that is becoming more important every day. As mentioned in Part I, enormous chunks of the world economy are already internationalized, and there is no sign that the trend is slowing down. Simply from the point of view of economics, therefore, we ought to have some understanding of this phenomenon.

Secondly, the multinational corporation has social and political implications which may be even more important than the economic ones. Charles Kindleberger makes these implications sound rather ominous: "The international corporation raises political problems, and especially problems of foreign policy, which political scientists have by and large ignored. Indeed, the international corporation may be said to threaten the nation-state . . ."[1]

A third reason for dealing with this subject is that it will give students a better understanding of America's role in world affairs. They will see that the international expansion of U.S. business is really quite different from the sort of extra-national exploits that occurred earlier in this century. The unit should also help them to understand why the peoples of the world seem to have such ambivalent feelings toward the United States, admiring and imitating her on the one hand, and tossing about inflammatory phrases like "American imperialism" and "Yankee Go Home" on the other.

[1] Kindleberger, Charles, Position paper delivered at U.S. Department of State Conference on the Multinational Corporation, Washington, D.C., Feb. 14, 1969, p. 5.

Fourth, this unit is designed to give students a better idea of what it means to look at the world as a system. They will see how the nation-state fits into this system, but that the world economy is really something quite distinct from a collection of national economies. Some comments by Kelman, at a recent conference, indicate the sort of understanding that should emerge from this kind of study:

> One of our major hang-ups is the tendency to think that the nation-state is the *only* form of organization to satisfy our needs. In some ways the nation-state has been good. It still may be good. That doesn't mean that the only alternative is some sort of global organization, but rather that for some purposes regional, cross-national and global organizations are better suited to our needs.
>
> Herbert Kelman, Speech delivered at Foreign Policy Association Conference on "Priorities in International Education," New York, Nov. 20, 1969.

Still another benefit of this study is that it will help students to see the Third World as a developing entity, with the individual nations involved being located at different stages along the continuum leading to modern industrial societies. They will learn something of the prospects and problems of developing nations by learning how the hopes and aspirations of those nations are intertwined with the activities of the global corporations.

Finally, this particular topic seems ideal for an inquiry unit. Except for the work of a very few economists, and some recent articles in periodicals, the information available in this field has not been thoroughly sifted and analyzed. The students, therefore, will be exploring an area where the data have not already been predigested for them.

Some Background

Before plunging into the task of creating a study unit on the multinational corporation, it would be better to have a pretty clear idea of what sort of phenomenon is being talked about.

First, do not confuse the multinational corporation with international *trade*. Exports and imports are involved, but the thing of primary interest here is the firm which carries on major portions of its total business operation in more than one country; the firms, in other words, which "build plants, staff them, and produce goods in countries other than their own." [2] This is what is called the "internationalization of production," and it includes service industries (banking, accounting, advertising, and so on), in addition to manufacturing and the extraction of resources.

Some examples will help:

1. IBM has factories and offices in 106 countries; the head of its World Trade division is a Frenchman and most of its overseas employees are not Americans; roughly one-third of the company's revenues comes from overseas operations; IBM is "big" in lots of places besides the United States—its share of the computer market in France, for example, is 66%. [3]

2. Ohrbach's department stores have outlets in California and New York, staffed by Americans, but its board of directors is located in the Hague and most of its stockholders are Dutch.

[2] Rolfe, Sidney E., *The Multinational Corporation*, N.Y., Foreign Policy Association, Headline Series No. 199, 1970, p. 4.

[3] Redding, William M., Jr., "The New Multinational Managers," *Saturday Review*, Nov. 22, 1969, p. 35.

3. International Telephone and Telegraph has its main office in New York, but three of its four research branches are in other countries, foreign production is equal to production in the United States, and its stockholders come from dozens of countries.[4]

4. The Italian automobile firm, Fiat, is building factories and training workers in the Soviet Union for the manufacture of cars that will be sold in the Soviet Union.

This list could be extended for dozens of pages, with American-based firms being the most numerous, but with many others, mostly European, appearing far from in-

The Internationalization of Production: IBM in Istanbul
Photo Credit: IBM World Trade Corporation

[4] Rolfe, Sidney E., *The Multinational Corporation*, N.Y., Foreign Policy Association, Headline Series No. 199, 1970, p. 8.

significant. We've already mentioned the important role these firms play in the economy of the world, and a glance at Tables 1 and 2 should make it even more evident. Note particularly, in Table 2, the percentage of world production that is contributed by the multinational businesses.

Table 1

U.S. Direct Investment in Other Countries, 1929–1966 (in billions of dollars)

Area	Year			
	1929	1946	1957	1966
Canada	2.0	2.5	8.6	16.8
Europe	1.4	1.0	4.1	16.2
Latin America	3.5	3.1	8.4	9.9
Africa & Middle East	0.1	0.2	**1.8**	3.7
Other Areas	0.5	0.4	2.6	7.9
Totals	7.5	7.2	25.5	54.5

U.S. Department of Commerce, *U.S. Business Investments in Foreign Countries.*

Table 2

Projected Growth of "Internationalized Production" (in billions of dollars)

	1968	1978	1988	1998
Output associated with U.S. investment abroad	200	450	950	2000
Output associated with foreign investment in U.S.	90	200	425	900
Non-U.S. corps, in other areas of the world	130	300	600	1300
Total output from international business	*420*	*950*	*1975*	*4200*
World GNP	1800	2900	4800	8000
% of GNP associated with internationalized production	*23%*	*33%*	*41%*	*53%*

Judd Polk, Chief Economist, International Chamber of Commerce.

Of course, this cross-national development of business has been going on for quite some time (although the big thrust has occurred since World War II), but for some reason few people seemed to realize just how important it was becoming. Until this past decade, literature on the subject was practically non-existent. In the past two or three years, however, a rapidly-growing body of materials has developed as economists, businessmen, and journalists attempt to assess precisely what is happening and where it might be leading.

From the point of view of teaching about global concerns, the global corporation provides a number of intriguing questions. What, for example, is the impact of these firms on the social, political, and economic institutions of the host country? This question is developed more fully in the unit itself, but it might be pointed out here, by way of illustration, that the biggest selling book in Europe for this generation is *The American Challenge,* a readable, non-technical analysis by a French journalist, J.-J. Servan-Schreiber, who feels that American-based global corporations threaten the independence of Europe. In the Preface to the American edition, Arthur Schlesinger, Jr., describes how serious the challenge looks to many Europeans.

If present tendencies continue, the third industrial power in the world, after America and Russia, could be, not Europe, but American industry in Europe. The present European generation has only a few years to decide between restoring an autonomous European civilization or allowing Europe to become a subsidiary of the United States.

Arthur Schlesinger, Jr., Preface to *The American Challenge,* by J.-J. Servan-Schreiber, N.Y., Atheneum House, p. ix.

A number of other topics would be exciting to investigate: the benefits the global corporation brings to the host country; the role of these firms in the developing nations; the advantages and problems of cross-cultural interaction, as people from different countries have to learn to live together and work together; the problems of controlling these businesses, since they don't come under the regulation of any single government; the rights of a host country to nationalize a global corporation's holdings within its borders. Some of these topics will be found rephrased as discussion or inquiry questions on pages 108–10.

Although economists are troubled by the scarcity of statistics on international economics, there are sufficient data for your purposes, and a growing volume of periodical literature is available. A sample list of recent (and readable) articles is on pages 110–13. As with the issues of global economy, students will find much of the literature to be interesting, stimulating, and quite free from the sort of professional jargon and statistical manipulation that might scare them off.

One final thought: economists, now in the process of catching up with the developments we've been discussing, are having considerable difficulty agreeing on precise definitions. Different economists use different yardsticks in trying to determine precisely what constitutes a multinational corporation. Your students will be quick to see that, for their purposes, a variety of labels can be used interchangeably: e.g., *multinational, international, extra-national, trans-national,* and *global* or *world* corporations. Incidentally, the technical term for establishing a business in another country is *direct investment.* Whatever labels are employed, be sure that students use them precisely and consistently.

The Unit: Suggested Procedure

First Day

Introduce students to the topic and explain why it is an important one. A rephrasing of the introduction to this chapter might be sufficient. More imaginative and interesting would be to develop a short picture study— most major corporations would be happy to supply you with pictures which would vividly illustrate the phenomenon. Discussion questions should follow:

1. Why do you think American firms want to start businesses in other countries, rather than just exporting to those countries?

2. Why would European firms want to do the same thing here?

3. Where do you suppose most multinational corporations would decide to go—to the developed or the underdeveloped countries? Why?

4. Why would a country want to have a foreign business within its borders, rather than having a domestic firm do it?

5. What reasons can you think of that encourage large American firms to build plants in different regions of this country? Would the same reasoning apply to building plants in other countries?

6. How do you suppose people in host nations react to the arrival of an American business? How would you feel if you were working for an Italian, or a Japanese, or an English company in the United States?

Of course the class won't be able to supply very sophisticated answers to these questions, but they should keep the questions in mind as they read. If the teacher is inquiry-oriented, the tentative answers might be reworded as hypotheses.

The assignment should be at least one magazine article for each student; you might make the selection from the Bibliography at the end of this chapter, concentrating on those that seem likely to offer a general description.

Second Day

Discuss again some of the questions from the previous day; point out ways in which hypotheses or views have been modified by reading or discussion.

On the basis of their reading so far, see if they can make a list of the advantages and disadvantages accruing to the host country, writing the lists on the board. (Again, this can be used as an exercise in hypothesis formation.) Discussion questions should follow:

1. If you were the prime minister of a European country, would you allow an American firm to build on your territory? Why or why not? What sort of conditions would you establish if you did agree?

2. Would you feel differently if you were the prime minister of a newly independent African nation? Explain.

3. If you were the president of an American company, what problems would you expect to encounter in an overseas operation? For example, how would your workers in this country react? What difficulties would you expect in terms of language and customs?

If the teacher prefers, these questions can be used as the basis for role-playing sessions; or you might make use of local sources who could add some personal insights—such as local businessmen or Peace Corps returnees.

The assignment can be based on as intensive a use of outside sources as the teacher desires. Ask students to write an essay on the advantages and disadvantages of the multinational corporation, supporting their arguments with factual information.

Third Day

This class period could be most profitably used to continue exploring the research topic, either through class discussion or individual conferences.

Fourth Day

Read to the students—or have them read from the original sources—the three accounts given here on the possible significance of the multinational corporation. They might keep these questions in mind during the reading:

1. Can you describe, in a sentence or two, the position taken by each of the authors?

2. Which of the accounts seems to you to be most valid? Explain.

3. Does your essay agree with any of these readings? Explain.

4. Do you find that the position you took in your essay has been modified or changed by these readings? Explain.

Reading No. 1

The nation-state has tried to build an international system for its own salvation but has always failed. Its commitment to absolute sovereignty has impeded its ability to contrive an extra-national body which would submerge and limit the state. If we live by the experience of the past, the modern nation-state cannot build an extra-national body to its own undoing as a nation-state bent on security above all else.

The second "sovereignty" is the extra-national corporate body. It is growing in number, size, influence, power, functions and independence. Excepting for the very great powers, the smaller nations are increasingly dependent upon the extra-national corporate body for the means of economic development, if not for survival. These corporate bodies are service organizations that perform their essential functions for a fee—such as interest on a bank loan, or a profit on oil distribution. They are a-political but possess great political influence if not political power. Their international character makes them indifferent to local political squabbles. Their supra-national structure places them beyond the need for national security so essential to the state. They have one great vulnerability.

Clearly, if the state manages to blunder into a holocaust which consumes the races of men that people the earth, then the international corporate bodies will go down the stream and be washed away as if they had never existed. But if we assume that life is carried by some creative impulse that will not die, that man has always contrived a new structure when the old one was worn out, when it could no longer provide for, and protect those whom it was meant to serve, then one would expect what has happened in the past to be repeated in the present impasse. The extra-national corporate body would seem the logical basis for the contrivance of a non-military supra-national order.

This is a strange destiny for the corporation. But primitive instances of it have been seen in the past: the Knight Templars and the Hanseatic League, for example. These functioned well for a time within the boundaries of the then known world. The reduction of the earth to the size of a large ancient parish with many autonomous governments makes the supra-national corporate body the natural bond between them. The speed of communication, the increased mobility and proliferation of the sciences make corporate organization increasingly evident, necessary and inevitable.

An industrialized world is held together by the large number of corporate bodies, and by their widening role. The corporation groups the nations into a new loyalty—

a functional identity across all borders. The day may well come when the majority of people in all nations will have their functional loyalties to one or more supra-national bodies. They may well become conscious of basic commitments, values and interests unrelated to the state or the nation.

This is probably inevitable if the industrial and technological upheaval works its way as it seems bound to do. The international corporate bodies would have differences with other similar organizations. But the differences would have little to do with nationalism or military security. What seems implicit in this development is a new supra-national order based not upon the state obsessed by security needs but resting on the naturally extra-national bodies that are visibly enveloping men and states over a large portion of the globe.

Time is the essence of change and transition. How long will it take for the corporate body to be so evidently the international structure as to make the formal legal organs contrived by the nation-state irrelevant because the state itself will become irrelevant to international dealings? It took many centuries before the commercial revolution gradually evolved a middle class that found the feudal order unacceptable and gradually contrived the nation-state to serve its ends. One cannot assume that so profound a structural change as here envisaged can go on without political implications, and without a shift in political power. It is difficult to see the way this shift of political power will occur—but that it will take place there can be no doubt. It would have been equally difficult to foresee the modern state in the glories of a feudal society.

How long will it take? Will the nation-state hold on long enough to permit this to occur or will it destroy itself and mankind as well? What about Russia and China? The answer here, I think, is clear. If Russia and China are going to become industrialized in the sense that the United States is industrialized, then they will go the same way—the international corporate body will reach over into the closed state as in some measure it already does. The international corporate body is a natural functional institution and it can only be kept from its role if there is no extensive industrial development. In either case the closed communist or the non-communist states will either destroy each other or persevere long enough to allow the unforeseen growth of the international corporate body to take on the requisite political role and bypass the problem of security while leaving to the state the police powers for internal civil needs.

This is the major issue confronting mankind. It is a question of time and no one can say whether man will allow himself the mercy of surviving long enough to find a way of transferring international political powers to the corporate bodies that have come into being unwittingly and whose commitments are primarily functional, to render service where it is needed—indifferent and untroubled by the issues of national security and sovereignty.

From "The Survival of the Fittest," by Frank Tannenbaum, *Columbia Journal of World Business,* March-April, 1968, p. 13. Reprinted by permission.

Reading No. 2

". . . Starting with a matter-of-fact examination of American investment in Europe, we find an economic system that is in a state of collapse. It is our own. We see a foreign challenger breaking down the political and psychological framework of our societies. We are witnessing the prelude to our own historical bankruptcy.

At times like this we naturally think about reinforcing the barricades to hold back the invader. But purely defensive measures might well make us even weaker. In trying to understand why this is so, we stumble across the key element. This war—and it is a war—is being fought not with dollars, or oil, or steel, or even with modern machines. It is being fought with creative imagination and organizational talent. . . .

Those whose job is to provide leadership and help us make decisions have been casually looking at each individual piece of the puzzle. Now it is time to concentrate on the problem as a whole. This strange phenomenon, dangerous and massive in its size and power, is so hypnotizing and overwhelming, that it threatens to plunge us from our present ignorance into total despair.

The day may indeed come when we can only sit by helplessly and watch Europe disappear as a center of civilization. But that day is not yet here, and there is still time to act.

Act how? Fight against what? We have less to fear from the absence of a European will than from its lack of direction.

General Motors, after all, isn't the Wehrmacht. The fight for the ownership of Machines Bull isn't Munich. And the supersonic Concorde jet isn't the battle of Sedan. This is the modern war, to be fought without arms or armor. If we had another Andre Malraux today, he would tug our heartstrings not with tales of the heroism of the fighters of Teruel, but with the fabulous struggle for the conquest of titanium, or the ferocious effort to master the mental world of integrated circuits.

Even without a great lyric poet to recount them, the facts themselves are charged with power and emotion. It is enough to watch American investment skim gently across the earth like the fabled swallow, and watch what it takes away, how 'it thrusts, twists, enfolds, tears away, carries off, breaks open, and attacks.' Here it comes.

From *The American Challenge,* by J.-J. Servan-Schreiber, published by Atheneum, and reprinted by permission of the publishers.[5]

Reading No. 3

The provision of material abundance is the business of business. Whether publicly or privately owned, local or global in nature, business organizations are the social instruments with the demonstrated capability and adaptability to pour forth an ever increasing flow of the goods and services that make possible—but do not necessarily assure—the 'good' life. Now . . . a new role for business is being shaped by far-reaching changes in the structure of world commerce. Comparative advantage is less a matter of geography than of superior technical knowledge and service efficiency. As the importance of resource endowment diminishes and that of knowledge and service increases, the logic of localized production and marketing becomes inescapable. The stage is set for the emergence of business organizations that, ideally, are dedicated to pursuing profits anywhere in the world and are not necessarily limited by identification with a given national home or particular operational headquarters.

Thus, great manufacturing and trading companies are becoming multinational at a faster pace than is sometimes realized. And, concurrently, they have developed a vast interwoven network of reciprocal interests, of open communications for exchange of technology and commercial intelligence, of personnel and of cultural patterns—even of new friendships and loyalties that cut across national boundaries. The multinational company thereby has become a major vehicle to carry the have-nots toward "take-off" and the haves into frontier fields.

Yet despite the benefits they promise, these new world enterprises have not had an easy time. Major difficulties arise from the continued strength of nationalistic committees, attitudes inherited from a feudalistic past, and political distrust of private motivations in many areas. No uniform global regulatory machinery has been devised, and it is hardly inconceivable that some marginal businessmen will take advantage of situations unprotected by competition, local laws, or established habits of rectitude. They always have.

Still, the emergence of the multinational corporation has brought a new and profoundly important influence to bear in world affairs. For global companies, unlike political entities, operate in an environment in which their negotiations do not carry a heavy baggage of emotional commitment, but in which the resolutions are most often mutually beneficial to both parties to the transaction. They provide a network of interconnected conduits that facilitate optimum utilization of financial and technical resources. Indeed, these multinational corporations that have developed so quietly, but so suddenly, may be the hoped-for force that will ultimately provide a means of unifying and reconciling the aspirations of mankind—a task which all the politicians have utterly failed to achieve.

From "A New World Symphony," by Courtney C. Brown, editorial in *The Saturday Review,* Nov. 22, 1969, p. 56. Reprinted by permission of Saturday Review, Inc.

Discussion based on the questions listed above should follow these readings.

Additional Questions

For the sake of illustration and flexibility, the procedure we've just described has been trimmed down to the point of superficiality. For above-average students, or for teachers who would like to make the study more thorough, we are adding a list of questions that can be used for additional discussion, research assignments, or inquiry exercises. Some of these questions could be woven into the unit outline above, while others would require additional research.

A. Placing the Multinational Corporation in Historical Perspective

1. What was the historical pattern of extra-national business activities in the early years of this century? How did host populations respond?

2. In what ways have the character and methods of the global corporation changed since World War II?

3. To what extent do these firms employ host populations? What is the relationship of employees to the firm; e.g., what percentage are in top management positions?

4. Why do some writers refer to the sudden and

rapid growth of global corporations as "the second Industrial Revolution"?

5. What industries are involved in this development? How important is global business to the U.S.; what percentage of GNP comes from overseas business?

6. Why have industrial countries, like England and France, accepted U.S. firms on their soil?

7. Explain why the success of global firms is said to depend on "the degree to which we see the world as an international economy instead of seeing it as a group of national economies."

8. What are the major obstacles to continued growth of multinational corporations? What projections are made about future growth?

B. The Multinational Corporation and the Third World

9. Are there any data to suggest that multinational corporations are helping either to close or to widen the gap between "rich nations" and "poor nations"?

10. What special problems face the global firm in Third World countries; e.g., availability of capital markets and skilled labor?

11. Examine the reactions in one Latin American country to American businesses and try to explain the reasons for reactions such as "Yankee go home."

12. To what extent does the host country share in the profits?

13. What is meant by the term "culture shock," and how do these firms cope with it?

14. What is the attitude of the radical left to the penetration by global businesses into developing countries? See, for example, Fanon's *The Wretched of the Earth*.

15. Examine the issue of nationalization as it has occurred in one country (e.g., Bolivia), and explain the arguments for and against such actions.

16. To what extent do international corporations drain

off the skilled people in Third World countries? See, for example, Adams' *The Brain Drain.*

BIBLIOGRAPHY

BOOKS

Adams, W. T., *The Brain Drain* (N.Y., The Macmillan Co., 1968).

Blaustein, Arthur I. and Woock, Roger R., (eds.), *Man Against Poverty: World War III* (N.Y., Random House, 1968).

Drucker, Peter, *The Age of Discontinuity* (N.Y., Harper & Row, 1969).

Fanon, Frantz, *The Wretched of the Earth* (N.Y., Grove Press, 1968).

Gabriel, Peter, *The International Transfer of Corporate Skills* (Cambridge, Harvard University Press, 1967).

Kenen, Peter B., *International Economics* (Englewood Cliffs, N.J., Prentice-Hall, 1967).

Kindleberger, Charles P., *American Business Abroad* (New Haven, Yale University Press, 1969).

The Multinational Corporation, Highlights and background papers of Conference held at the Department of State, 2/14/69, Office of External Research, Dept. of State, 1969.

Pincus, John A., *Reshaping the World Economy; Rich Countries and Poor* (Englewood Cliffs, N.J., Prentice-Hall, 1968).

Rolfe, Sidney E., *The Multinational Corporation,* Headline Series No. 199 (N.Y., Foreign Policy Association, 1970).

Rolfe, Sidney E., (ed.), *The Multinational Corporation in the World Economy* (N.Y., Praeger, 1969).

Servan-Schreiber, J.-J., *The American Challenge* (N.Y., Avon Books, 1969).

Ward, Barbara, *The Rich Nations and the Poor Nations* (N.Y., W. W. Norton & Co., 1962).

ARTICLES

Ball, George W., "Toward a World Economy," *Dun's Review,* February 1968, p. 19.

Benham, Joseph, "In Latin America: Growing Threats to U.S. Companies," *U.S. News and World Report,* July 14, 1969, pp. 68–70.

Diamond, Robert S., "Managers Away From Home," *Fortune,* August 15, 1969, pp. 56–58.

Heilbroner, Robert L., "The Perils of American Economic Power," *Saturday Review,* August 10, 1968, pp. 21–24.

Kraar, Louis, "Southeast Asia Builds for the Post-Vietnam Age," *Fortune,* August 5, 1969, pp. 76–80.

Lambert, John, "Brussels: The Executive City," *Dun's Review,* March 1969, pp. 48–51.

Lubar, Robert, "The Challenge of Multinational Business," *Fortune,* August 15, 1969, pp. 73–74.

Polk, Judd, "The Rise of World Corporations," *Saturday Review,* November 22, 1969, pp. 32–34.

Redding, William M., Jr., "The New Multinational Managers," *Saturday Review,* November 22, 1969, pp. 35–36.

Rose, Sanford, "Rewarding Strategies of Multinationalism," *Fortune,* September 15, 1968, pp. 100–105.

Vernon, Raymond, "What Strategy for the Third World?" *Saturday Review,* November 22, 1969, pp. 42–46.

"Brussels Sprouts: U.S. Companies Open European Headquarters in Brussels," *Time,* February 2, 1968, pp. 67–68.

"Spreading the System: Program to Train Foreign Students in U.S. Business Ways," *Business Week*, August 17, 1968, p. 84.

"NCR Makes Going Native Pay Off," *Business Week*, December 14, 1968, pp. 114–116.

"Does Overseas Investing Help?" *Business Week*, January 4, 1969, pp. 50–52.

"U.S. Agribusiness Shows the Way," *Business Week*, January 18, 1969, pp. 52–58.

"More Capital Goes Abroad," *Business Week*, August 9, 1969, p. 38.

"Nationalization in Zambia," *Time*, August 22, 1969, p. 72.

"Business Is Riding with the Irish Storm," *Business Week*, August 23, 1969, pp. 32–33.

"How U.S. Industry Is Remaking the World," *U.S. News and World Report*, October 27, 1969, pp. 58–60.

"Where Yanqui Companies Are Feeling the Heat," *Business Week*, November 22, 1969, pp. 80–84.

ADDITONAL SOURCES

As we mentioned in the text of this chapter, the teacher can find excellent resource people—e.g., Peace Corps returnees and local businessmen—within his own community. In addition, many corporations and business organizations offer good material at modest costs; here are some examples:

The National Planning Association has published a series of booklets under the collective title of *United States Business Performance Abroad*. These are quite readable and non-technical; some sample titles are: *Aluminum Limited in India*, by Subbiah Kannappan and Eugene W. Burgess; *The Case of the General Electric Co. in Brazil*, by Theodore Geiger; and *IBM in France*, by Boyd France. The Economic Research Division of Chase Manhattan

Bank, New York, N.Y., 10015 publishes a *World Business* quarterly.

The First National Bank of Chicago, Chicago, Ill., 60690, releases a monthly *International Economic Review.*

A little searching will undoubtedly turn up many other sources. Although some of the following may be too technical or scholarly, a careful review will reveal a number of items that would be of interest to the students as well as the teacher:

The Columbia Journal of World Business, Columbia University, New York, N.Y. 10027, a quarterly journal which produces excellent articles on the political and social factors as well as the economic ones. Several articles will be included in a forthcoming book published by the Macmillan Co. (Free Press) under the title *World Business: Promise and Problems.* We appreciate the help of Richard W. Greenebaum, Associate Editor, in locating material for this sample unit.

The International Chamber of Commerce, New York, N.Y., Judd Polk, Chief Economist, has a number of publications of interest.

The Joint Council on Economic Education, is particularly helpful to teachers. The Council's newsletter and bibliographies, as well as source material, are excellent aids to anyone whose teaching touches on economics. Our thanks to Miss Evelyn Schwartz for help in locating material.

3

Developing Global Units for Elementary Schools

Teaching about Spaceship Earth

DESPITE A SHINY NEW COVER AND BRILLIANTLY PICTURED pages, the textbook that continues to dominate the scene in today's one million elementary classrooms much as it did in the pre-Space days, takes a traditional approach to world affairs. With a greater need than ever before to perceive themselves and their fellow men as members of a single species and the world as a single system, Space

[1] By Donald Morris, Director of School Service, Boulder Regional Office, Foreign Policy Association.

Age children continue to have their perceptions limited and often distorted by text material that offers only an ethnocentric focus, presenting the world as a flat piece of real estate, the center of which is their home, their family, and their community.

To paraphrase George Leonard's words from *Education and Ecstasy,* it is too bad that no elementary textbook writers have been sky divers and that no designers of elementary curriculum have orbited the earth.[2] To view the earth physically detached from it might inspire them to design and provide materials and experiences to liberate young minds and cause them to see and perceive the pattern of the whole quilt before being confounded by the variety of patches.

Without completely revising textbooks, and without devising sophisticated curriculum materials, there is a great deal that the elementary teacher can do to help children begin to develop a global perspective, and at the same time make the classroom interesting and exciting. This will be especially true if you make use of one of your most valuable resources—the child's imagination.

You might, for example, use simple devices like the following—this one designed to get at the idea of the need to look at things from different angles or viewpoints:

Drop a penny into a glass bowl filled with water. Without blocking the view of the rest of the class, have one student, using a thin stick, yardstick, or whatever is handy, point to the penny. Then insert the stick at that same angle into the water until it touches the bottom of the bowl. It will seldom touch the penny and the stick will always (unless inserted straight down) appear to be broken or bent at the surface of the water. Older children with some experience in fishing objects out of ponds and

[2] Leonard, George B., *Education and Ecstasy,* (Delacorte Press, 1965).

streams will of course not be surprised by this phenomenon, but the point is still well taken.

Even in the area of science, where we can be relatively certain of our facts, we must be careful to make adjustments for such things as refraction in our visual perception. You can use this idea as a springboard to discuss how important it is to be careful in making judgments in other areas—like judging other people on the basis of limited perceptions such as color of skin, type of dress, or customs that seem strange to us.

Such discussions can lay the groundwork for the child in developing generalizations about mankind, and can be useful in moving him toward objectives identified in the Study, such as "developing an understanding of basic human commonalities" while also "developing an understanding of the sources of differences in human actions and life styles." (p. 102) In other words, if we can use examples of perception and misperception by directly involving the child in simple classroom exercises, we have a much better chance of helping him learn that human beings all have the same basic needs, but it is the variety of responses to these needs that are learned from the culture and which make them appear so different.

To introduce concepts such as the earth as a system and the interrelatedness of man, you can easily transform your classroom into a simulated spaceship. The pupils' imagination will help in this. Then read to them the following section, What Would You Do? You can carry this idea as far as you want to, but even an hour or so will bring important results.

What Would You Do?

Just for a moment, imagine that you are a first-class passenger on a huge spaceship with thousands of passengers travelling through space at a speed of 66,000 mph. You discover that the craft's environmental system is faulty. Passengers in some sections are actually dying due to the emission of poisonous gases into their oxygen supply. Furthermore, you learn that there is a serious shortage of provisions—food supplies are rapidly diminishing and the water supply, thought previously to be more than adequate, is rapidly becoming polluted due to fouling from breakdowns in the craft's waste and propulsion systems.

To complicate matters even more, in the economy sections where passengers are crowded together under the most difficult of situations it is reported that many are seriously ill. The ship's medical officers are able to help only a fraction of the sick and medicines are in short supply.

Mutinies have been reported, and although some of the crew and passengers are engaged in serious conflict in one of the compartments it is hoped that this conflict is being contained successfully; however, there is widespread fear as to what may happen if it cannot be contained or resolved within that compartment.

The spacecraft has been designed with an overall destruct system, the controls of which have been carefully guarded. Unfortunately the number of technologists who have gained access to the destruct system has increased, and all of the crew and passengers have become uneasy due to evidences of mental instability in some of those gaining such access.

We could go on, but the point is this: what would you do if you were put in such a position? Now that you have "imagined" this situation, are you ready to face reality? You are on such a spaceship right now—Spaceship Earth!

What are you going to do about it?

(This "Spaceship Earth" concept is developed more fully in the experimental unit described on pp. 120–31.)

Some Resource Suggestions

Although programs and lessons that facilitate the development of "world mindedness" as opposed to the "we-they" view are preferable, certainly the study of other peoples and other nations continues to be an important part of elementary world affairs education. As has been stressed elsewhere in this book, such studies must avoid the common error of providing only a superficial view of a nation, often out of context, which serves only to reinforce preconceived ideas and stereotypes. Here are some suggestions to help make the study of other peoples an experience in developing understanding and empathy.

First, make use of as much non-textbook material as you can manage: films, tapes, pictures, primary source material, artifacts, books from other English-speaking countries, educational games, simulations.

How can a teacher possibly assemble material from all of these sources for every country to be studied during the year? The answer is simple. You can't! But it would be far better to deal with fewer countries in some depth than to try to "cover" all of them in your textbook at a dangerously superficial level. Then study the balance of countries, as time permits, on a survey basis, validating the facts presented and the ideas implied by the authors by checking them against these other sources whenever possible. This is challenging to young people and it begins to develop patterns of thinking and inquiring into who is saying what and why they may be saying it a certain way.

Every school of any size which professes to deal with world affairs certainly should have, at a minimum, up-to-date copies of the *World Almanac* and the *United Nations Statistical Yearbook* from which to draw raw data for inquiry lessons. Of course, in lower grades, the teacher will have to extract the information and present it in small doses, using simple terms of comparison. For example, instead of referring to "gross national product per capita," you might say, "the average person in country A grows (or produces) twice as much as the average person in country B."

In addition to a variety of maps, your room should be equipped with a globe—the larger the better. A physical globe is preferable to a political one, and, if possible, it should be in relief. While not inexpensive, such globes are within the budget of most school systems. Edcom Systems, Inc. (145 Witherspoon Street, Princeton, New Jersey 08540) has a 30″ globe that is lightweight, non-breakable, and sells for just under $100. Even when using maps, you should refer often to the globe in order to minimize the distortions and limited perspective of flat maps.

With regard to materials and books from other nations printed in English, don't forget that Canada, Great Britain, Australia, New Zealand, and South Africa are not the only nations that have material you can use. India, Burma, Pakistan, Malaysia, and many new nations in Africa publish material in English. Note the advantages of such sources: you not only get the viewpoints of a particular country about itself, as reflected by the authorship, but viewpoints as well on a third country and even some ideas about the United States.

A number of international agencies offer a wide variety of material at little or no cost. UNICEF's Information Center on Children's Cultures offers annotated bibliographies, references on pictures and posters, and booklists. (331 East 38th Street, New York, N.Y. 10016.) UNESCO's

Division of Education for International Understanding has available, among other materials, a booklet titled *International Understanding at School* which reviews social studies programs in many countries, with particular emphasis on how one nation views another.

The material from OXFAM is not well known in this country, but here's a sample of what their Education Department offers: free monthly subscriptions to *OX-FAM News for Primary Schools*, inexpensive games, posters, paperbacks, and even do-it-yourself recipes if you want to put on a Bolivian, Korean, Greek, or international dinner. (OXFAM, 274 Banbury Road, Oxford, England.) If you have trouble translating dollars and cents into shillings and pence, your local bank or travel agent can give you an assist.

In addition to the simulations described earlier in this book, you might be interested in something a little different—culture-based games from different countries, produced by World-Wide Games, Box 450, Delaware, Ohio 43015. Simple and inexpensive items such as Pommawonga can be effectively used to introduce a discussion of how games have developed in many cultures to reflect the critical importance of learning certain behavior patterns and skills in order to survive.

Experimental Program[3]

In the summer of 1969, an experimental program was conducted at the Elementary Laboratory School at Colorado State College, Greeley, Colorado. A series of several

[3] By Peggy Herring, Audiovisual Coordinator, Woodmere School System, Woodmere, New York. This experiment was carried out by a team of consultants headed by Peggy Herring, with assistance from Donald Morris. The classroom programs were conducted with the cooperation of Dr. Boyd La Marsh in the classrooms of Dr. Marjorie Harkness and Mrs. Lelloine Gunning.

lessons was developed for third to fifth graders dealing with man, his environment, and their interdependence— lessons that reached toward learning to view the earth as a single system.

The overall objective was to expose the children to some awareness about people and the environment in which they live and to help them develop some concepts which might serve as yardsticks for measuring the importance of conditions, events, and actions, and which could provide them with a functional filing system for all the bits of information that constantly feed into their brains. A "value judgment" post-test administered to the students and video-taping of the actual lessons provided some accurate as well as rewarding retrospect regarding the effects of the experiment.

We are presenting the following description of portions of the program, not so much for purposes of replication, but to illustrate the application at the elementary school level of some of the concepts and approaches discussed in this book. For each of the three lessons we will give first the methods and objectives, and then excerpts from the classroom dialogue taken from the video tapes, which will give you some idea of the excitement, enthusiasm and important thinking with which the pupils reacted.

Lesson 1—Simulation—Living in a Spaceship

The first session was a simulation. The children were the passengers and crew on board a spaceship. Through the use of an overhead transparency, which projected a drawing of the inside of the ship, and an audiotape, the environment was established. As the group traveled through space, the audiotape dramatized a sequence of events that limited the air, food, and water supply and created problems with overcrowded conditions, all understandable situations with which the youngsters could identify. Periods of discussion during the simulation and following it permitted the children to participate actively and early in the lesson. They talked about the complications that could develop in a limited environment, about the need for cooperative efforts among people in close proximity to each other or dependent on each other, about the kinds of internal conflict which can arise when people are subject to discomfort, deprivation, danger, and other forms of stress.

There was excitement in the classroom. There were differing opinions and viewpoints. There was arguing. And, the biases of ten-year-olds were projected. Among the ideas most heatedly discussed were the effective use of a limited environment, resolving conflict, coping with varying aggressive behaviors in individuals and groups, decision making, formal and informal leadership roles. A base was being planted from which further examination and extension of these topics could develop. There were identifiable social realities, which ultimately could relate to the more abstract study of real forms of government, economics, world distribution of population, wealth, power, trade, or most any aspect of a social science curriculum—a fertile valley for plowing up ideas and exposing them to sunlight, air, and each other. No judgments, no "rightness" was imposed on any of the discussion—only further probing questions. The questions, a series of open-ended points relating to the various events occuring on the tape, were used to prompt children's responses and draw more elaborate reactions from them.

The specific objectives of this lesson were to have the children identify with what is essential for survival (specifically on a spaceship so as to bring the experience into a perspective with which they could empathize) and to begin to recognize the dependence of people on each other and on their environment. The children perceptively enough also saw that the survival of the environment depended on people.

Dialogue—Lesson 1—Simulation— Living in a Spaceship

(*The spaceship is far from any source of contact or replenishment. There has been an air supply failure in one compartment. The commander has limited the food and water to all passengers and some crew. Certain crew have been kept on full rations because of their critical job responsibilities. One compartment is temporarily overcrowded because another room is without oxygen. This is midway through the lesson.*)

TEACHER: How do these new problems with the environment affect you?

FIRST PUPIL: Well, we have to be careful about the food. If we waste any we'll run out before we can get more.

SECOND: I don't think it's fair that some of the crew should still be getting full rations. Just because they have to keep the ship running, it isn't fair.

THIRD: But if they don't, then more things could go wrong on the ship and then everybody might die . . .

FOURTH: Yes, but which jobs are the most important?

FIFTH: Maybe the passengers and the crew should talk about it together. Why should just the captain decide? Maybe he's got some favorite crew members and he just wants to treat them better.

SIXTH: No, he wouldn't do that.

SEVENTH: But if you let everybody say what they want, you could end up with a big argument. That's why you have a captain, otherwise everybody is arguing and fighting.

EIGHTH: Yes, they have to do what the captain says. He's supposed to know more about the ship and what to do. That's why he studied to be a captain.

NINTH: Well, what about all the people crowded in Compartment B. Why didn't the captain let some of them go into some of the other rooms?

TENTH: I sure wouldn't want to be in there.

SEVENTH: Pretty soon they will use up all the oxygen and that room will be no good either. And then they will all want to go someplace else on the ship.

EIGHTH: Then there won't be anyplace left to go.

ELEVENTH: Well the ship can't land anywhere. So we better work out something. What a mess!

TWELFTH: Maybe the crew will take over the ship.

EIGHTH: That's mutiny.

(*Another section of the tape—two crew members have stolen some extra rations from the storeroom.*)

TEACHER: If you're a passenger on this ship and knew about this, how do you think you would feel about it?

FIRST: That's not fair. It's dishonest.

SECOND: They weren't thinking about anyone else. And it just means the food will run out sooner.

THIRD: Then those crew members will be in the same trouble as everybody else—so it really didn't do them any good.

FOURTH: I think I might have taken some, too, if I was real hungry.

FIFTH: The captain should punish them, throw them in the brig or something.

SIXTH: No, let the passengers get their food for three days.

SEVENTH: Well, I wouldn't steal. It's not fair.

(*More comments along these lines*)

TEACHER: You can see that even among us there is some question as to what is right or wrong in a complicated situation like this. When people are under stress they may act differently than when they are calm. There also seems to be some indecision about what, if anything, should be done if the crew members are found out. Suppose you were the crew member, then how might you feel?

FIRST: (*child who thought the captain should punish them earlier*) Well, if we don't keep the ship running, then everybody gets in trouble, so we really ought to have plenty to eat.

SECOND: Maybe if my job was important enough, I would need the extra food.

THIRD: Anyway, if nobody finds out . . .

FOURTH: All the passengers have to do is ride along. They don't have to work. So they shouldn't have to eat as much.

FIFTH: That's not true. Just because you're not working doesn't mean you don't get just as hungry.

(*Summarizing comment by teacher at end of session*)

TEACHER: Let's remember how we thought and felt today about these situations. These same kinds of problems will come up again sometime, perhaps soon. They may be slightly different, but basically these are the kinds of problems which we may have to deal with as we live from day to day. What we have to keep in mind is how each of us saw the problems. We had differing feelings about them and differing ideas about how to attempt to solve the problems.

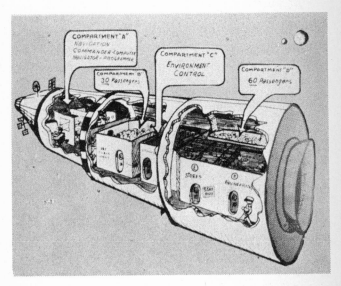

"Spaceship Earth" model for overhead projector

Lesson 2—Models—Demonstrating "Systemness"

The second session focused on working models to demonstrate the meaning of "system." The objective was to encourage the children to acquire some comprehension of the concept and characteristics of systems. Through individual and small group manipulation of flashlights, blocks, gear toys, and woven fabrics, and some questioning on the part of the teacher, the children saw and discussed the meanings of parts, whole, function, and relationship. Then a game of "tug-o-war" quickly helped to clarify the words interdependence and interrelationship.

After the children had talked at some length, trying to explain the models as systems, and using the vocabulary introduced to them until it was comfortable, a period of discussion followed. They were asked to think about systems made up of people (family, community, nation, school, scouts were mentioned), systems of ideas (language, music, mathematics, trade, government were among those discussed), and systems of things (transportation, telephone company were talked about).

With older groups, the concept was extended to the areas of economics, politics, science and various aspects of technology. As various systems were discussed and examined, some children offered comments on the differences between manmade and natural systems, those that were complete and independent, and those which needed other systems in order to function, some that were made of real things (concrete), and those that couldn't be seen or touched (analytical) but existed. The involvement and participation of the children in these sessions was extremely high.

Dialogue—Lesson 2—Demonstrating "Systemness"

(Individual children, or small groups of children, have been handling objects composed of several parts which won't work unless they are assembled together—example, a flashlight.)

TEACHER: What is this?

FIRST PUPIL: A battery.

TEACHER: And this?

FIRST: A bulb.

TEACHER: Will they work separately?

FIRST: No.

TEACHER: Why not?

FIRST: Well, you have to put them together. They have to work together.

(Questions relating to the words part, whole, dependent, function, system *as children develop the concept, while manipulating the various models which they have been given.)*

TEACHER: Can you think of other kinds of systems in which people or things depend on each other?

FIRST: We just studied the digestive system in science.

TEACHER: How is that a system?

FIRST: Well, there are all these parts, you know, the stomach, and the intestines. And they digest your food. And if you don't have all the parts, then you'll get sick. The stomach does one thing and the next part does something else.

(Other pupils describe nervous system, circulatory system, blood system, music system, money system, numbers, etc.)

TEACHER: Can you think of systems in which people are the parts?

SECOND: When people live together, like in a city.

THIRD: And then you have to have laws. That's a system. Otherwise everybody would be doing what he wanted to do.

FOURTH: That's why we have a president, and policemen, and judges, and government, and things like that.

TEACHER: Are all those things you mention systems or parts of systems? Do they affect other systems?

(*Multiple answers in response to inquiry.*)

TEACHER: How do we understand each other? How do we communicate?

FIRST: We talk to each other. We use words.

SECOND: Or we use sign language.

THIRD: Braille, blind people use braille. That's a system.

FOURTH: Our classroom is a system. We're the parts and we have to act a certain way or everything would be a big mess.

(*More discussion extending the systems concept into other areas and emphasizing their interdependence.*)

Final Sessions—Earth as a Spaceship and Earth as a System

Final sessions pulled together the seemingly disconnected insights transferring the "living in a spaceship" identification to "living on spaceship earth."

A transparency illustrating a real environment was projected and children were asked to identify the essentials of any environment for staying alive. This was a simple transfer of the learning in the spaceship lesson. Another transparency illustrating the earth as a composite of several systems—air, water, land, etc.,—was projected and children discussed the interdependence of these systems. One by one each system was removed from the earth to see if the earth could exist as a total system. As will be noted from the dialogue, their answers were astonishingly revealing in terms of how much learning input they had stored up, ready for this kind of reasoning and inquiry.

Following this large group discussion, the children were given experimental materials to work with in small groups. A raised relief map of the world, a baster, and some clear water were the beginning. The children "rained" on the world and watched the water flow from mountain top, to stream, to river, to lake, to bigger river, to ocean. They watched water flow from the Pacific and meet the Atlantic. They saw the connected water system of the world. A second step using an eye dropper (to slow down the process somewhat for observation purposes) and polluted water (white tempera diluted) involved the children in polluting the water system of the world.

They tried polluting just one small isolated stream and observed how eventually, using enough polluted liquid, this polluted stream reached everywhere. Even if it flowed down the Mississippi, the pollution eventually reached the Amazon, or the Nile.

The next experiment used a constellation globe (which has a clear plastic earth inside a large clear plastic globe) and a miniature fire extinguisher. The same concept regarding the world's air system was illustrated as children tried to pollute the air in only one part of the world. The experiment quite vividly illustrated the point as the outer globe filled completely with the small blast of "polluted air." The enthusiasm of the children as well as the kinds of discussion that were generated after these experiments revealed that a tremendous amount of sound learning was occurring in the classroom.

Dialogue—Lessons—Earth as a Spaceship and Earth as a System

TEACHER: Let's just take away all the plant life on earth, the trees, the grass, the plants. They're all gone. What might happen?

FIRST PUPIL: We need the trees and plants for food.

SECOND: No we don't. We still have animals and fish,

so we can have plenty of meat and milk. That's all we need.

THIRD: But some of the animals live on plants. What will happen to them?

FOURTH: They would die. And eventually we would all die.

FIFTH: Also the plants and trees have roots. They hold the soil and rocks. Pretty soon the land would all wash away.

SIXTH: Besides, a lot of animals and birds use trees and bushes for protection from the rain and snow.

SEVENTH: And if the land gets all washed away, where would the animals live?

EIGHTH: What about the air. Green plants turn carbon dioxide into oxygen. (*A long and thorough explanation ensued as this youngster proudly revealed his science knowledge.*) We would use up all the air.

NINTH: You can't take the plant life away. It's important.

TENTH: Yes, we need it to survive.

TEACHER: All right, we'll leave the plants. Let's try using up all the mineral resources in the world. No iron ore left, no oil, or coal, no copper, and so on.

FIRST: But we use a lot of iron—like in buildings.

SECOND: And we make steel from iron for lots of things.

THIRD: Yes, like bridges and cars. How would we get around?

FOURTH: And airplanes and ships.

FIFTH: What would happen to trade? We couldn't ship anything and people couldn't send us things from other countries.

SIXTH: And what would happen to the stores? They have to have stuff to sell. And nearly everything is made of iron or steel or rubber or stuff like that.

SEVENTH: No it isn't. We have lots of plastic.

EIGHTH: Well, my father has a plant and they make all kinds of iron bolts. What would he do if there wasn't any iron left?

NINTH: Lots of people would lose their jobs.

TENTH: And there wouldn't be any trucks to **drive**.

What would the truck drivers do?

ELEVENTH: How would we keep warm in the winter if we didn't have coal or oil?

TWELFTH: Pretty soon we would burn up all the trees for fuel.

THIRTEENTH: We wouldn't even have a place to live.

FOURTEENTH: There wouldn't be any telephones.

FIFTEENTH: Or schools.

CHORUS: Hurray.

EVERYBODY: (*Laughter*) . . .

TEACHER: Let's consider those pollution experiments we did. What did you learn from them?

FIRST: Well, what you do on one side of the earth will go to the other side.

SECOND: And what they do on the other side will come over here.

THIRD: And if it's something bad, we don't want it to happen.

FOURTH: It's like on the spaceship. You have to take care of the system.

TEACHER: Do we have a responsibility to people in the other parts of the world?

CONTRIBUTORS TO AN EXAMINATION OF OBJECTIVES, NEEDS AND PRIORITIES IN INTERNATIONAL EDUCATION IN U.S. SECONDARY AND ELEMENTARY SCHOOLS

Dr. Judith Torney
College of Education, University of Illinois
Chicago, Illinois

Dr. Harry Targ (Assisted by Natalie Morgan)
Department of Political Science, Purdue University
Lafayette, Indiana

Mr. H. Thomas Collins, Director
Division of School Services, The African-American
  Institute
866 United Nations Plaza, New York, N.Y.

Dr. Frank H. Klassen, Associate Secretary
American Association of Colleges for Teacher Education
One Dupont Circle, N.W., Room 610, Washington, D.C.

Chadwick Alger
International Relations Program, Northwestern University
Evanston, Illinois

Kenneth Boulding
Institute of Behavioral Science, University of Colorado
Boulder, Colorado

Robert Harper
Department of Geography, University of Maryland
College Park, Maryland

Bruce Joyce
Department of Curriculum and Teaching,
Teachers College, Columbia University
New York, N.Y.

Herbert Kelman
Department of Psychology, University of Michigan
Ann Arbor, Michigan

Robert LeVine
Committee on Human Development, University
  of Chicago
Chicago, Illinois

Charles McClelland
Department of Political Science, University of California
Los Angeles, California

Howard Mehlinger
High School Curriculum Center in Government,
  Indiana University
Bloomington, Indiana

Robert North
Studies in International Conflict and Integration,
  Stanford University
Palo Alto, California

Kenneth Prewitt
National Opinion Research Center, University of Chicago
Chicago, Illinois

Readings

Reading no. 1, by Kenneth Boulding, is from Social Education. *His article, "Education for the Spaceship Earth," explains and attempts to deal with the problem of passing on
to today's students an ever-increasing body of knowledge and
an awareness and understanding not only of their own society
and culture but of universal human activity, the superculture.*

*Reading no. 2, "Some Problems in Improving International
Education" by Chadwick Alger, calls for a change in our habit
of teaching international relations from an ethnocentric point
of view. This article is also from* Social Education.

*Contemplating the near future, considering in particular
environmental resources, population increase, and technological change, Robert C. North weighs the hopeful and dis-*

couraging prospects. "The World of the Forthcoming Decades: A Pessimistic and Optimistic View" is the third reading from Social Education.

In "A Basic Framework for Social Sciences: Two Fundamental Human-Earth Equations and their Juxtaposition," Robert A. Harper, the author, defines two ways of examining man and his world: 1) by dividing the earth into many locally-based culture groups and studying each as an entity; 2) by considering the whole world as an interconnected system and studying the universal aspects of man. Harper explains the importance of both approaches in teaching social studies today.

These readings are all reprinted from a special issue of Social Education (Nov., 1968) *devoted to the study.*

Education for the Spaceship Earth

BY KENNETH E. BOULDING

The "noösphere," as Pierre Teilhard de Chardin calls it, is far and away the most important aspect of the world social system.[1] This is the sphere of cognitive structures or images as they exist in the minds of men or even in non-human structures. A central purpose of the "knowledge industry" as Fritz Machlup calls it[2] is to transmit

---

[1] De Chardin, Pierre Teilhard, *The Phenomenon of Man* (New York, Harper and Row, 1961).

[2] Machlup, Fritz, *The Production and Distribution of Knowledge in the United States* (Princeton, N.J., Princeton University Press, 1962).

the noösphere from one generation to the next as well as to expand it and make it correspond more and more with "reality," whatever that is. It is a slightly terrifying thought that all human knowledge is lost approximately every generation by the processes of aging and death and has to be replaced in new bodies. If this process of transmission were interrupted even for 30 years, the human race would revert probably to its paleolithic condition, or might even become extinct.

Formal education, that is, the process which goes on in schools, colleges, universities and other "firms" of the knowledge industry, is only part of the total knowledge industry and only part of this great process of transmission. As the human being grows from birth to adulthood, he learns a great deal from the simple observation of the world around him through his senses. He learns a great deal also from his peers and in his family, mostly from oral communication; and in these days he learns a great deal from the television and the radio. Once he has been taught to read, mainly by the agencies of formal education, he can learn a great deal by reading outside the processes of schooling. Nevertheless, the noösphere of the modern world is so large and so complex that it requires a large formal educational establishment to transmit it. This establishment, furthermore, grows larger all the time and absorbs an ever increasing proportion of the gross national product, partly because as knowledge grows continuously, more effort is required just to transmit it from one generation to the next; partly because education is a technologically unprogressive industry and so the price of education continually rises relative to other commodities.

The noösphere consists not merely of images of the world of objects; it also contains images of values, both those of personal preference which we call tastes and those preferences which we feel apply beyond ourselves to other people and which we call ethical systems. Ethical systems, that is, shared values and preferences, are an essential part of community. A culture or a subculture can be defined as a group of people holding certain value systems in common, and a community is simply the organizational expression of a culture. A vital part of the transmission process, therefore, is "socialization"; that is, the feeding of inputs into the growing child, largely of information and symbolism, which will turn him into a member of "his" community. It is this process which turns Chinese children into Chinese and American children into Americans. In this process formal education plays a role at least as important as that of the family and the peer group. Thus as the church transmits a religious culture from its present adult members to their children, so the public school system of all countries is a kind of "church" of the national state, socializing the child into becoming a citizen of a particular country in which he grows up.

Herein lies one of the great dilemmas of the world today and especially the dilemma of international education. Because of what has happened in the field of technology, especially of transportation and weaponry, in the past few decades, the world has become a "spaceship," a small rather crowded globe hurtling through space to an unknown destination and bearing on its surface a very fragile freight of mankind and the noösphere which inhabits men's minds.

Conflict Between Old and New World Views

This represents a very fundamental change in the condition of man, a change which, furthermore, only a few people have really appreciated. Until very recently the human race was expanding on what was for all practical purposes an illimitable plane. It may have been "a darkling plain . . . where ignorant armies clash by night," as Matthew Arnold called it, but it was for all practical purposes an illimitable, if rough, plane. As long as there was always somewhere to go over the horizon, neither ignorance nor armies nor clashes could be fatal. If one civilization collapsed another one could always rise a few hundred miles away. All history, in other words, until very recently, has been local and has not involved the concept of the "sociosphere" or the total sphere of all human activity extending all round the earth. It is now almost a cliché to say that the world has become one and it has become small. The real implications of this, however, are very far from having been realized. The kind of organization, ethic, and conduct which may be quite appropriate to a great plane are quite inappropriate for the crowded and precarious conditions of a spaceship. The great problem of this generation is precisely to provide a symbol, an ethical code, and an organizational structure which is appropriate to this extraordinary transformation in the real condition of mankind.

Here the system of formal education finds itself caught in a very painful dilemma. On the one hand, it is formal education, especially at the level of the university, which has mainly created the spaceship and destroyed the great plane. Science, it is true, originated and developed largely outside of the structure of the formal university. Nevertheless, today it is the university which is the principal agent of transmission and expansion of the body of scientific knowledge, and it is this body of knowledge which has created the jet plane and the nuclear weapon.

It is not surprising, therefore, to find an increasing tension between the university as a community and the rest of society which supports it, simply because the university is the representative of what I have elsewhere called the "super-culture" and is primarily engaged both in expanding the superculture and transmitting it to the next generation. In many respects, however, this superculture is in sharp conflict with the ideals and the images of the folk culture or the local culture around it which still retains the attitudes and the images which are appropriate to the great plane. The worldwide student unrest is perhaps only one symptom of a larger conflict between the whole university community and the local societies in which it is everywhere embedded, whether these are Communist or capitalist, traditional or modern, for even the most modern of societies contain very large elements of the folk and local culture out of which the superculture has grown.

On the whole this conflict between the superculture and the local cultures has not yet penetrated very far down into the high school and the grade school from the universities. Nevertheless, insofar as the universities produce the teachers in primary and secondary schools, or at least produce the teachers of these teachers, the tensions between the whole educational industry and the society around it may be expected to grow, at least for one more generation.

Resistance to the Spaceship Earth Concept

International education is all too likely to be the focal point of this conflict. On the Great Plane we can play cowboys and Indians; and it is even appropriate to develop local societies, or nations, which build their identity largely around contrast with and opposition to the neighboring nations around them. The appropriate value system and image of the world under these circumstances is highly ethnocentric, looking at the world in sharp perspective from the capital city of the nation and developing a value system in which the nation is highly sacred, demands and receives sacrifices of human life, as well as liberty and treasure, and finds its highest expression of community in war. It is not surprising, therefore, that in primary and secondary schools everywhere national anthems are sung, pledges to flags are repeated, and the portrait of the reigning ruler or president is frequently displayed prominently. Furthermore, the curriculum is designed to glorify the national state, geography is taught in a perspective manner with the home country prominently studied and displayed, the national boundaries are firmly printed into the consciousness, and foreign countries are treated as distant and reduced in size. In history and social studies, likewise, the history of the home country is glorified and the histories of other countries are neglected. National school systems indeed are not above a good deal of falsification of history in the interest of creating good citizens. In the study of literature, similarly, the native language, except in colonial countries and regions, receives prime attention and other languages and literatures are regarded as "foreign." Only science in the curriculum can be regarded as a universal element. Even here the achievements of native scientists may be prominently displayed and the foreign scientists underplayed.

Any attempt to introduce what might be called a spaceship earth education, therefore, will be regarded with extreme suspicion. Wherever the curriculum of formal education impinges on images of the world which the local culture around it treasures, sensitive areas are set up which are avoided as far as possible. Religion, race, and nationalism, as has already been noted, are among these areas; and the study of the international system almost inevitably impinges on all of them. It is not surprising, therefore, that international education tends to follow the innocuous patterns of interesting stories about strange children, and any attempt to teach the international system as a total system might easily run into very serious criticism for the defenders of the local culture. This is precisely because what might be called international systems education, to distinguish it from more innocuous brands, deliberately sets out to destroy the illusions of perspective and to point out the things at a distance are not really small, still less are they unimportant. We can still, however, concede a great deal of realism in the proposition that the near are dear. Moral perspectives of this kind are not only realistic but are not incompatible with the systems point of view.

Those engaged in formal education, therefore, are always walking an uneasy tightrope. On the one hand, it is easy for them to violate the sensibilities of the older generation, especially those in the folk culture, who after all largely pay their salaries. On the other hand, the educator who does not "tell it like it is" is in great danger of being found out if the image of the world which he is propagating to his students does not correspond to what they are going to discover in their subsequent life experience. If a student finds that teachers have deceived him and have taught him things that are not so, the whole sacredness, prestige, and legitimacy of the teaching profession is threatened. My own case is an example. My formal education was heavily weighted with messages designed to turn me into a good little Englishman. In adolescence I read H. G. Wells's *Outline of History*, which persuaded me that my teachers, especially my history teachers, were liars; and largely I think as a result of this, I eventually became an American. If our children find out that their teachers are liars, or at least supersititious and gravely in error, the consequences to the whole socialization process and the very fabric or society itself could be

disastrous. Some of the current revolt of youth, especially
of students, may very well be related to the fact that the
pablum which they get in primary and secondary schools
is so unrelated to the realities of the world today that it
proves indigestible.

View from the Moon

The critical question of international education, therefore, is whether we can develop an image of the world
system which is at the same time realistic and also not
too threatening to the folk cultures within which the
school systems are embedded; for if educators do not find
a palatable formula, the "folk" will revolt and seek to
divert formal education once again into traditional chan-
nels, as for instance in the famous anti-evolution laws of
Tennessee and Arkansas or even some so-called "economic education." A possible approach to this problem is
to take advantage of the new image of the world that is
a consequence of the exploration of space in which, for
instance, the act of viewing the earth from the moon
clearly reveals it as a ball floating in space and makes
very clear the closed nature of the sphere. From the vantage point of the moon, the facts are so clear that it should
not be too difficult to organize a whole curriculum around
the concept of the earth as a total system, including of
course a certain amount of astronomy to put earth in its
setting in the solar system, the galaxy, and the universe.
The inputs to the earth from anything outside except
the sun are so minute—in terms of energy, though not in
terms of information—that from the point of view of
earth as a system we can virtually neglect them.

We could continue, then, with geomorophology and
the study of the lithosphere, the hydrosphere, and the

atmosphere as total systems, always constantly moving towards an equilibrium which is equally constantly disturbed. Then, of course, we go on to the biosphere, which should be taught mainly from the point of view of world ecology, stressing its interdependence with the other systems but stressing also the concept of the ecosystem on both the micro and the macro scale. The time dimension would constantly be introduced to give an evolutionary perspective both in the study of inorganic and organic forms so that the student is introduced to the concept of development in biological evolution. From this it should be an easy transition to the sociosphere and to human history and to geography, beginning with the geography of the paleolithic and prehuman hominoids, going on to the neolithic, and then to shifting and expanding patterns of civilization. The problem of time perspective is particularly difficult here. The near is interesting as well as the dear, and what is near in time and space is of more interest to us than what is distant. Nevertheless, there must be some kind of uneasy compromise between the anti-perspective view which regards the present moment and the present location of the student as a very small sample of an enormous totality stretching through time and space and the perspective view which frankly asks the student to look back into time, forward into the future, and out into space from where he is at the moment. It was one of the real strengths of progressive education that it could capture the interest of the student by starting from where he was. On the other hand, if the education process leaves the student there, it will have failed in its essential function, which is precisely to destroy the illusion of perspective and to enable the student to step outside of himself and see himself as a point (or rather something like a four-dimensional worm) in the enormous space-time continuum of the universe. Hardly any problem relating to education is trickier than this.

Problems of Teaching the International System

When we come down to the study of the international system proper as a segment of the total sociosphere, the dilemma of perspective becomes even more agonizing. From the anti-perspective point of view the international system is seen as a total globular system of over one hundred national states, a variety of dependencies, a cluster of international organizations, both governmental and non-governmental, plus the international corporations, and so on. A great deal of what is ordinarily taught in the history books is the history of the international system or at least of a segment of it. It has been only within the last four hundred years that the system has become truly global in its extent. It is only in the last generation it has become a real "spaceship system" in which war is becoming increasingly intolerable and dangerous, and in which the international system itself because of its inherent stability is tending to gobble up an increasing proportion of world resources and income—resources which in the present critical stage of human development can very ill be spared.

One of the great problems of international education, whether at the adult or at the school level, is the absence of any clear image of the dynamics of the international system and particularly of any dynamic process which would lead towards an alternative system which is superior to what we have now. It is very hard to teach what we do not know, and the awful truth is that we do not know very much about the international system. The theory about it is very inadequate, the information system from which we derive our images of it has a built-in tendency to produce misinformation, and on the whole the decision-makers in the international system are dominated by what might be called "folk images" approximately at the level of the flat earth.

A very important element in the subconscious attitude toward the teaching of the international system is a widespread fear that the international system must move toward world government and the destruction of existing national sovereignties. There is indeed a fair amount of propaganda to this effect by the World Federalists and like-minded people. This is similar to the often largely subconscious fear that any discussion of religion will lead to the loss of faith or any discussion of economics will lead to socialism or any discussion of race will lead to racial mixtures. All these fears are deeply ingrained in the folk cultures of this country and in some form of all countries, and furthermore they cannot simply be dismissed as irrational, although they all have strong irrational elements in them.

It is very important, therefore, for the teachers and researchers in the international system to have an image of the future which does not necessarily involve either total catastrophe, or a reversal of the developmental process, or the destruction of existing national states and their total absorption into a universal world culture and polity. Just as we are beginning to see domestically that the more complex a society, the more pluralistic it can afford to be, so we ought to be able to see in the international system that a system is possible which both preserves the national state and is capable of stable peace. The critical question is, What are the dynamic processes by which this happy state is achieved?

Up to now the body of what might be called received knowledge in the international system has not really faced up to these problems, though the work of writers like John Burton[3] in England and myself in this country suggests that solutions to the problem of war are possible short of world government and not inconsistent with the preservation of local and national cultures and organizations. If this view could become widespread, even as a kind of orthodox synthesis between the views of the status quo "realists" who think the present international system can survive, which I think is an illusion, and the world government advocates whose solution is much too radical and frightening to receive much acceptance, we might finally have something to teach which would be acceptable, both to the scholars and to the lay public. Here again we must stress the tremendous interconnection between teaching and research because again we cannot teach what we do not know.

It is shocking that there is no word for the science of international systems. One would like to suggest Xenoology (from the Greek *xenos*—foreign) on the grounds that the international system arises precisely because some people regard other people as "foreign." This would be indeed the science of generalized foreign affairs. Perhaps there is not enough yet to teach. Nevertheless, I am optimistic enough to think that in the last generation at least we have developed both a body of theory and the beginnings at least of a systematic collection of information which make such a science conceivable.

Preparation of New Teachers and New Materials

This raises the question, however, when we have something to teach, who will teach the teachers? This perhaps is a one-generation lag which we can very ill afford. The

[3] John W. Burton is the author of *International Relations* (New York, Cambridge University Press, 1966).

"new economics" of the 1930's is only now beginning to penetrate the secondary schools. The new international politics or Xenoology would have an even thornier path to tread before it got anything like general acceptance. It may well be, therefore, that we do need to think in terms of the whole program and of how the student and the teacher may be prepared to accept a total curriculum based on the spaceship earth.

Here the preparation of learning materials may be as important as the preparation of teachers themselves. Every child should certainly have a globe, and there must be ways of making him brood over it with the ambition of reaching some sort of geographical closure; that is, knowing roughly at least where everything is. One would like indeed to see the principle of the spelling bee applied to simple geography so that it becomes, as it were, a kind of sport to know who everybody's neighbors are. The desire for closure, for knowing everything about something, that produces for instance the spelling bee and the passion that many twelve-year-olds have for knowing the averages of all baseball players throughout history is something that we have inadequately exploited in our educational motivations. Geography, of course, could be a beautiful case of it, simply because the map of the world is now virtually complete. History is more difficult because of the added dimension. Nevertheless, a fairly substantial investment in good historical atlases would go a long way towards correcting the fallacies of perspective, especially if these, too, were printed on globes. What I would like, indeed, would be a globe for every year of human history printed so that it could be explored with a microscope and so that the student, for instance, who wanted to know the history of, shall we say Northern Italy in 1316 would simply go to the corresponding globe and examine Northern Italy with a microscope and find the history printed there. One could do a great deal also with movies that zoom from outer space to show the setting of any particular event. Devices like these might encourage a learning process both in teachers and students which would be very far-reaching. In a way the computer may have done us a disservice by diverting our attention from these simpler and more static devices because of the intoxication with the manipulation of numerical data. This, too, has its place, however; and the development of games and simulation should not be neglected.

It could well be that the next fulcrum from which the earth might be moved will be the teachers colleges and the universities which have grown out of them but which still specialize in the training of teachers. A program in the international system for the teachers of teachers would have a multiplier effect and could bring about quite rapid change.

Finally, of course, there is the good old book, still the backbone of education of all kinds, in spite of audiovisual and computational aids. Here the need is for a pioneering book which will attempt to convey, especially to the high school student, the sense of excitement, the sense of wide new horizons and the sense of world reconstruction which is going on now among the students of the international system. Whether a book like this can be commissioned I do not know. It might be worth a try or we may just have to wait for it. The need for a book of this kind is so great, however, that one can hardly believe that the supply will not be forthcoming.

We cannot predict exactly what form the book—or books—is going to take. We can, however, visualize several characteristics. It will involve essentially an image of the international system which includes a developmental dynamic just as the image of the economic system now includes a notion of economic development. The great advantage economists have is that in measures like real income per head we have a single scalar measure which at least gives us a good clue as to whether we are going up or down. In the international system it is often very difficult to tell whether we are going up or down. A measure of the "tone" of the international system as a whole, derived perhaps from the content analysis of public utterances, would carry us a long way toward the image of a developmental dynamic. A developmental dynamic in the international system, however, implies that we know at least vaguely where we want to go. Here, as I have suggested earlier, a dynamic which moves in the direction of stable peace among relatively independent nations seems to be much preferable in the present state of affairs than a dynamic which moves toward a world state, even less a world empire. The fact that we have already established stable peace in segments of the international system (for instance, in North America and in Scandinavia), suggest that a dynamic process which leads toward stable peace among independent nations already exists. At the moment, however, we are not self-conscious about this and we do not direct our teaching of the international system in this direction. In North America, for instance, I have been arguing that we got stable peace as a result of a succession of lucky accidents; for instance, the Rush-Bagot Agreement of 1817, the settlement of the Oregon boundary at the forty-ninth parallel (we didn't get 54° 40′ and we didn't fight), the British non-intervention in the Civil War, and so on. History is not taught, however, emphasizing these turning points or, as I have sometimes called them, hurdles.

Theory of the Dynamics of Stable Peace

I have attempted to develop a theory of the dynamics of stable peace along the lines that it is something like a hurdles race: if the doves win three times we are "in"; but if they lose any one time, we have to go back to the beginning and start over again with a threat-counterthreat system. Up to now, therefore, stable peace has developed largely as a result of lucky accidents. If, however, we can get a self-conscious notion of the process and direct our teaching accordingly, we could produce national policies aimed at increasing the probabilities of stable peace. At the moment we do not really have such policies. We still regard peace and war as "political meteorology," just as we used to regard depressions as "economic meteorology." I remember, indeed, when the Great Depression was called an "economic blizzard." At the moment our teaching of history is completely the other way—it is designed to reinforce the image of unstable peace. Thus, as I travel around the country speaking, I frequently ask audiences if those who have heard of the Rush-Bagot agreement would raise their hands; the score is rarely more than about 2 percent. Yet it could be argued that this is one of the most important events in American history and that without it the First World War would have been fought between Britain and the United States and could easily have taken place in the Middle West. Perhaps what is needed is a commission of historians, political scientists, strategists, peace researchers, and so on to study the problem of the dynamics of stable peace as it has developed, especially in the last 150 years, with a view perhaps of developing a small textbook in this area. Or perhaps, as committees have such a poor record in literature, at least since the King James version of the Bible, we must hopefully wait for private enterprise to match the demand with a supply.

Some Problems in Improving International Education

BY CHADWICK F. ALGER

Education can liberate or imprison. Much that is called international education is of the latter kind. Images of the world of the past and preoccupation with certain current events filter out much of the world of the present. This almost makes it impossible to think realistically about the future. Several problems stand out as causes of our inability to grapple effectively with international education of the kind needed for our students to live productive adult lives in the twenty-first century.

Preoccupation with United States Foreign Policy

Much of what is taught about international relations is done in the context of United States foreign policy on certain issues of great concern to the United States. This gives students a view of the world as perceived from one nation—and a very large one. A way must be found to put these issues in the context of the whole, as several of the papers in this issue of *Social Education* indicate. This will require a curriculum that views the total system—not only from a vantage point outside of a specific nation but also from a vantage point outside the nation system itself.

Problems of Change

The world is undergoing rapid change. How we study the world also is changing rapidly. This sets the basic context for thinking about the international education of children and adolescents.

Many of us are tired of hearing clichés about change. We are familiar with population curves that reveal that world population has risen from 0.5 billion in 1650 to 2.5 billion in 1950, a fivefold increase in three hundred years. It no longer seems startling to be told that this 2.5 billion will double before 1990. We are familiar with similar curves for speeds in intercontinental travel, rising from 25 to 1,000 miles an hour in less than a century. Also familiar is the steep curve showing the destructiveness of weapons. But familiarity with a few statistics on change is one thing and adequate response is quite another. International education curriculum has not yet adequately taken into account the potential consequences for the United States, and for the nation system itself, of dramatic changes in population, transportation, and the destructive power of weapons.

In international relations we have often exhibited a tendency to take change into account only up to the present time and to assume implicitly that the world will continue without further change. Our adaptation to the bipolar world is an example of such behavior. Taking into account the rapid changes in international relations that followed World War II, many writers, often implicitly rather than explicitly, tended to assume that this pattern would prevail—if not forever, at least for a long time. While focusing on the Cold War aspects of a bipolar world, often we have been unable to perceive fundamental changes taking place elsewhere, particularly in the new nations. As we approach the end of a century, there seem to be a number of efforts to make predictions for the next 32 years. This may be a sign that we are now developing the capacity to handle future change as well as that of the past. All international curricula should include discussion and prediction of the future.

Accordingly, each course and each textbook ought to include sections on the future, including specific predictions. Subsequent courses and textbooks should then analyze these predictions, in order to learn the causes of error. Predictions should include descriptions of expected technological change and changes to be expected in human behavior, such as travel, communication, use of leisure, etc. These changes should be examined in terms of the agenda of problems they will produce and the problem-solving institutions that will be required to handle these problems.

Students might be encouraged to design alternative international institutions to handle problems that they anticipate will be important on future agendas, such as pollution of the seas, militarization of the seabed, and wars over claims to the resources on the seabed. These could be designed in problem papers or in simulations. This might prevent images of the problems and institutions of today, and yesterday, from imprisoning the minds of those whom we are trying to prepare to anticipate the problems of the future and to design institutions to solve them.

The simultaneous occurrence of the twentieth century revolution in social science compounds the difficulty of curriculum development in international education. This includes not only radical change in methods of data collection and analysis but application of theory across fields formerly isolated from each other—for example, application of the same integration theory to both metropolitan and international politics. Thus, customary divisions of knowledge are being rejected, with important consequences for curriculum planning.

It will become increasingly difficult to plan an international education curriculum separately from other curricula. It is now not uncommon to hear discussions of violence that include both domestic and international phenomena. In discussions of problems created by the division of societies into the rich and the poor there are increasing references to both national and international examples. Furthermore, rigorous analysis is causing us to define more precisely our terms, including terms such as nation, which we apply customarily to such divergent entities as the United States, the Congo, and Malta. Developing theory and precision in definition may produce, therefore, divisions of knowledge that cut across our customary international relations category.

Continuing change in both the world we study and in the way we study it are important considerations for curriculum planning in international education. Not only must international change be a key concern in the curriculum, the curriculum itself must have a built-in capacity to change. A curriculum that might be regarded as perfect today may be a distinct liability tomorrow without built-in provisions for taking into account changes in the world, changes in analytic techniques, and the development or refinement of theory.

Problems of "Self-Analysis"

National loyalty is not the only kind of loyalty to inhibit realistic analysis of social issues, but its effect may be the greatest. The strong moral tone of the United States foreign policy objectives appears to generate an extreme self-righteousness that inhibits detached evaluation of United States performance by its citizens. This phenomenon is quite evident, for example, in attitudes of citizens, including many officials, toward United States perform-ance in the United Nations. United States policy state-ments, opinion polls, and the like reveal that the United States supports the United Nations with great moral fervor. But United States performance tends not to be carefully measured against this standard. It is generally assumed that the United States lives up to these moral principles. Different standards are applied in evaluating United Nations statements by "us" than are applied in evaluating statements by "them." For example, speeches by "them" are often treated as "nothing but propaganda," while speeches by "us" tend not to be labeled in this way. "We" may be different, but students tend not to be en-couraged to take an analytic posture that will enable them to find out for sure.

While teachers develop more explicit and effective techniques enabling students to make detached analyses of international relations situations in which the United States is involved, they need not destroy nationalism and loyalty to country any more than as a child learns that his parents are fallible, he need love them less.

The student would learn, then, a new role—that of detached observer and analyst, consciously separate from the role of loyal citizen. One very useful beginning tech-nique for encouraging an analytic posture is to abolish use of the pronoun "we" in the classroom when reference is being made to a nation or groups of nations. Students should be assigned tasks of policy evaluation according to certain prescribed standards either chosen by them or assigned.

The Big Nation Syndrome

Self-analysis may be more difficult in a giant nation, where most citizens are distant from any border, use only one language, and where most citizens get virtually all of their information from media produced by their nation. Considering what is to be found on the newsstands of many European cities, the differences between the *Chicago Sun Times* and the *Chicago Tribune* seem insignificant. Most American organizations are so big and consume so much energy in coordinating and running themselves that they have little time or energy to devote foreign counterparts. However, in smaller nations more citizens are near a neighboring country and less satisfied with and dependent upon national media. National organizations are less able to serve fully the activity and information sought by members.

It is necessary that teachers make students self-conscious of the constraints that life in a big nation places upon information from abroad and opportunity for foreign experience. This should include efforts to provide sensitivity to the perception of big nations by small nations. For example, United States citizens are very concerned about the fact that they have only one vote in the United Nations, although they provide 40 percent of its income and are a superpower. But it is important for Americans to empathize with the feeling of powerlessness to shape events that citizens of small powers have and their feeling that their nation often must cast its vote the way a superpower dictates.

In addition, it is necessary for citizens of big powers to be sensitive to differing standards for measuring contributions to international enterprises. For example, although most Americans are disturbed that their nation— only one of over 120 nations in the United Nations— contributes 40 percent of the budgets of the United Nations family, most do not know that the United States ranks twentieth in per capita contributions to the United Nations.

The "Nation" as an Analytic Blinder

The maps with national boundaries from which we initially learn about the world generate assumptions about human behavior from which it is difficult to free ourselves—in thinking about both actual and potential patterns of global behavior. There are linguistic maps, occupational maps, physical maps, etc., but none shapes our view of the world so much as the political map. Our view of the importance of nations also is affected by the way in which various actors use national symbols. For example, in hundreds of agencies around the world individuals are speaking with signs in front of them saying "United States." Although they represent different agencies of government, and often contradict each other, we tend to treat them as though they were all one person. Arnold Wolfers points effectively, however, to phenomena overlooked by this perspective:

> Some democratic states have exhibited such pluralistic tendencies that they offer to the world a picture of near-anarchy. They seem to speak to the world with many and conflicting voices and to act as if one hand—agency or faction—does not know what the other hand is doing. . . . [In] some . . . new states . . . integration is so poor that other states must deal with parts, rather than with a fictitious whole, if diplomacy is to be effective.
>
> Arnold Wolfers, "The Actors in International Politics." *Theoretical Aspects of International Relations* (Notre Dame, Ind., University of Notre Dame Press, 1959), p. 102.

Wolfers' observations raise serious question about our tendency to treat nations as single actors. For example, on the basis of whatever definition of "major" we might choose, does it make any difference how many major individual actors nation "X" has in the system at one time?

Does it make any difference where they are located and to what kinds of issues they are assigned? Would other nations be more effective if they dealt with the United States as one actor, or would they be more effective if they related to the United States as a number of actors? To what extent was *a* United States revealed in the events of the U-2 affair? When the officials of a nation involved in international relations are numbered in the thousands and sometimes tens of thousands, and are in all parts of the globe, coordination of their activity into something resembling that of a single actor may be a goal but it is only partially realized. The difference between the goal and degree of achievement may be a significant factor in international relations.

The political map also may influence our lack of attention to non-territorial groups and organizations that cut across national boundaries. For example, why have we neglected to include international business corporations in our international studies? Some have more influence on international relations than many international organizations and nations about which we require our students to learn. Some have annual budgets that surpass the total budgets of all intergovernmental and nongovernmental international organizations, and also surpass the budgets of many nations. Corporations, such as Shell, Nestlé, Coca-Cola, and IBM are encountered around the world. Some international corporations have activities in, and officials from, so many nations that it is difficult to assign them a single nationality.

Inadequate Models of World Order

When people think about the desirability of peace in the international system, they tend to base their thinking on analogies from experience in their own nations. If they live in a reasonably peaceful nation with a strong central government, such as the United States, they tend to believe that it is the government that is responsible for peace. Therefore, they believe that we cannot have world peace without world government; and they also tend to believe that this government ought to look something like their own government. But this line of reasoning overlooks the possibility that national governments are as much a result of already existing peaceful conditions as a cause of such conditions. It also does not take into account the likelihood that world government would develop out of the melding of a variety of governmental patterns and international conditions rather than follow the customs of any one nation. Furthermore, the assumptions that a world government is necessary for world peace neglects the fact that many nations have had peaceful relations, in the present as well as in the past, without world governmental institutions.

Whatever formal intergovernmental institutions might be deemed necessary to achieve a desired kind of international community, there are indications that researchers and prophets should be paying more attention to international *non*governmental and business organizations. The role of nongovernmental groups in the domestic political system of nation-states may be suggestive of their meaning at the international level. For example, recent research on developing nations has tended to emphasize the importance of social organizations to the development of a viable political system. Almond and Coleman[1] in *The Politics of the Developing Areas* stressed the importance of nongovernmental groups—labor and business organizations, political pressure groups, etc.—that link individual wants to governmental decision making. With-

[1] Almond, Gabriel, and James Coleman, *The Politics of the Developing Areas* (Princeton, N.J., Princeton University Press, 1960).

out such a political process, in which nongovernmental groups are crucial, even the best of governmental institutions may not be able to perform this vital role in a society.

It is reasonable to think of nongovernmental international organizations as having the potential for fulfilling the same function in the international system. Indeed, Haas has drawn attention to the way in which trade associations and trade unions in Europe have organized across national lines in order to lobby for their interests in the European Economic Community.[2] For example, the steel producers throughout the Community have organized in order to lobby in the EEC institutions against some of the pleas of a similar organization developed by steel workers. In this way controversy over certain economic issues is transformed from conflict between nations to conflict between international groups. The EEC institutions become more vital as they become the arena in which such disputes are waged and sometimes resolved.

Which Agency Can Handle the Problem?

The key problem in local, national, and international politics is deciding which agency can best handle a problem. Sometimes an agency is given a task without adequate thought about the appropriateness of the task for the agency. An example would be the attempt by the Department of Defense to sponsor a large-scale social science research project in foreign affairs called Project Camelot.[3] Some think that national military establishments, particularly their nuclear arsenals, such as those

[2] Haas, Ernst, "The Challenge of Regionalism," *International Organization* 12 (1958):440–458.

[3] Horowitz, Irving L., (ed.), *The Rise and Fall of Project Camelot* (Cambridge, Mass., Massachusetts Institute of Technology Press, 1967).

built by the United States and the Soviet Union, do not serve their intended goal—peace—as well as other kinds of military forces or entirely different kinds of institutions.

Students can see near their homes how agencies once adequate for certain jobs are no longer effective. This is particularly obvious in metropolitan areas where separate communities must band together, creating new agencies for handling police, transportation, or sewage disposal. Those who live on the Canadian border may be aware of the numerous agencies that perform functions that cut across the U.S.-Canadian border, and may become sensitive to the limitations of strictly national institutions for handling some problems. But most of us tend to accept the performance of functions by the nation without ever pondering whether international agencies might perform them more effectively. Although it is often asserted that international organizations can implement more effectively technical assistance programs, they are still minute compared to bilateral programs. The slight use of international agencies is reflected in the total annual budgets of the United Nations and all the specialized agencies: $580,000,000. This is less than the budget of many U.S. corporations and is, indeed, small when compared to the U.S. annual budget of some $30,000,000,000 for Vietnam.

If policy makers are to have the flexibility they need in assigning problems to international agencies and in creating new agencies when needed, it will be necessary for international education to encourage future citizens and and future policy makers to focus more on problems and less on institutions. It is our present tendency to teach how certain institutions—community government, national government, the United Nations, etc.—handle already assigned functions. Curriculum could be organized around problems in such a way that it highlighted more effectively the shortcomings of institutions and, most importantly, emphasized problems for which no effective decisional unit existed. This might enable students to develop habits of problem allocation that are based less on emotional loyalties—such as loyalties to city and nation —and more on the basis of criteria dictated by effective problem solving.

A View of the World Agenda

In planning international education for the coming decades the United States can gain valuable experience by assessing the failure of education during the past several decades to prepare its citizens for the problems of social change the United States is facing today. Why do so many Americans think the answer to violence in Watts, Detroit, Chicago, and Newark is better police? Why do they look to military power to solve problems in Vietnam? Why do they look upon the United Nations primarily as a peacekeeping agency? Do they realize that the citizens of most nations are more anxious about what the United Nations can do to give them better food, shelter, and clothing than they are about the improvement of U.N. peacekeeping forces?

Part of the difficulty in handling both domestic and international violence is our inflated notion of the capability of military and police forces to produce order. This has been discussed already above. But another part of the difficulty is caused by the limited knowledge that policy makers and citizens have of the total agenda of problems of national and international societies. Even the white liberals most sensitive to the problems of the blacks are only beginning to appreciate fully the total impact of segregation on the blacks in terms of deprivation of education, jobs, equal justice, etc. Many Americans still believe that corrective action is simply rewarding the undeserving and lazy. They look in the same way upon pleas on the part of the deprived nations in international assemblies.

It is vital that international education place the things that the United States most wants from its international activities—mainly peace and stability—in the context of the wants of all mankind. What is the composite agenda of items that people around the world believe ought to be handled by some kind of international activity or international agency? The varying hierarchies of priority around the world ought to be portrayed vividly. How well are agencies such as the United Nations doing in regard to these felt needs? Why are they doing so very little? Will lack of achievement internationally, which seems to be paralleling past lack of achievement nationally, bring results similar to Watts?

The World
of the Forthcoming Decades:
A Pessimistic and Optimistic View

BY ROBERT C. NORTH

In building conjectures about the world and the unfolding of international relations in the forthcoming decades, we are confronted with three broad considerations—environmental resources; numbers and densities of population; and levels of technology. In a sense, the future can be viewed as a close race between population growth, on the one hand, and the increasing capacity of people, on the other hand, to harness the environment effectively and to achieve sufficient wisdom soon enough to manage conflicts peaceably and use technology constructively.

Given man's record to date, the potentials for world conflict are staggering. But human beings have the capacity to pursue rational solutions if they choose to do so. However, tasks of the magnitude of those which confront us require considerable lead time for effective solutions. Even if the population brakes were slammed on world wide tomorrow—an unlikely, virtually impossible occurrence—it would require many years for the full consequences to be realized.

The task is at once political, economic and technological. It is also social and psychological. But technology in a broad sense—the organization and application of human knowledge, skills and tools—provide us with unprecedented alternatives and opportunities, provided we can learn fast enough to make timely and adequate use of them. Unfortunately—but inevitably—these unfolding technological developments can be used to save mankind and enhance his creativity and possibilities for self-fulfillment; or to increase his misery and even to bring about his self-destruction.

Among ongoing technological revolutions with a capacity for profoundly altering the lives and fortunes of all mankind are: (1) nuclear power and weaponry; (2) space explorations; (3) satellite networks with capacity for providing "instant" verbal and visual communications over much of the earth; (4) supersonic transportation bringing all major cities of the world within less than an hour's commuting distance of each other; (5) cybernetic systems with possibilities of controlling industries, communication and transportation, urban services, tax allocation and collection, voting arrangements, police records, and the like and of contributing to and vastly enhancing engineering, architectural planning, urban development, diagnosis of disease, bioengineering, space and ocean exploration and development, and so forth; (6) the prolongation of life, the enhancement of specialized functions by surgical implantation and electronic supplementation, manipulation of genetic structure, and the creation of life itself.

Virtually every one of these developments can be viewed as having positive consequences or negative consequences or—more probably—a combination of both. A mapping of extreme possibilities might look something like this:

Optimistic

World-wide, consensual, pluralistic but effective international control and institutions for resolving international disputes—possibly with decentralized regional units for regional conflicts. Universally sanctioned countervailing measures for heading off disorders and potentially dangerous confrontations—some economic, perhaps other social or political or judicial. National armed forces as out of date as private armed forces are today—armies, navies and air forces (if they exist at all) having become a carefully controlled and safeguarded monopoly of the international peace-keeping institutions for the preservation of international law, order and justice. Military technology converted for ocean and space exploration and colonization and other constructive enterprises on a vast international scale.

Pessimistic

Cataclysmic nuclear, biological or radiological war. Or proliferation of more conventional and less, devastating but nevertheless destructive and disruptive wars on land, on sea, in the air, and in space. Or generations of cold war; nuclear or other blackmail from military bases in space; ideological warfare through control of communication satellites. Proliferation of conflicts along a single or a few lines of cleavage; e.g., the richer, securer, advancing, healthier, longer-living, and less prolific whites versus the poorer, less secure, slower developing, less healthy, shorter-living more prolific coloreds.

Optimistic

Population levels carefully regulated by region in accord with available resources and levels of productivity. Loosening of national barriers to allow free flows of travel and immigration is correlated with inducements to attract populations where a labor force is needed or where the environment can support larger numbers of people. World-wide opportunities for advancement on basis of inherent capability and without restriction with respect to race, creed, color, and perhaps nationality. Rational, world-wide intercontinental, inter-cultural and international programs for agricultural, economic, technological and scientific development. Industries seek their functional environments, but non-industrial regions enjoy equal access to industrial products—and without undue additional cost.

Pessimistic

Vast uncontrolled population increases, coupled with continuing pollution and exhaustion of resources—at least in some parts of the world. Travel and immigration strictly limited from economic necessity and fear. Rich nations getting richer, poor nations getting poorer; within nations the well-to-do majority gaining while the depressed minorities become more depressed. Wars of "liberation" in underdeveloped areas and endemic guerrilla conflicts threatening to escalate.

Optimistic

Internationally regulated visual and audio communications networks serving as a world-wide free and open marketplace for news, information, knowledge, and culture. Strict safeguards against possibilities for monolithic control by a single nation or a few.

Pessimistic

Cybernetic control of visual and audio communication networks around the world by a single autocratic power or two or three deeply antagonistic superpowers.

Optimistic

Division and dispersion of governmental decision and control—according to function—on local, provincial, national, regional and world-wide levels. World-wide, international functions limited to the keeping of world-wide peace; international economic, technological, scientific, and communications regulation and development; international space exploration and control. National autonomy with respect to national affairs which do not impinge on the welfare and security of other nations. Considerable provincial and local autonomy wherever such autonomy is functional or calculated as desirable to counterbalance the power and authority of the national government. Computers programed to perform routine administrative functions and reduce top-heavy bureaucracies. Vastly increased citizen participation in local and even national governments.

Pessimistic

Supergovernments (or super-industries, religious, benevolent and protective associations, or crime syndicates) controlling—with cybernetic aids—tax levying and collection, police surveillance, education and indoctrination, political and/or religious belief without countervailing pressures and protections available to individuals and small groups; dictatorships with almost instantly retrievable master files and dossiers for each of its citizens with vital statistics, intelligence and aptitude quotients, personality profiles, school credentials, employment records, tax status, law violations, record of memberships, associations, incautious remarks, indiscretions, etc. Also, governments or professional groups with the knowledge and power to lengthen or shorten life, tamper surgically or genetically with human minds and bodies.

Optimistic

As cybernetics and automation take over more and more of the repetitive tasks of society, the educational system enhances the capacities of citizens to participate in the arts (painting, sculpture, music, literature, theater, dance, motion-picture making), science (experiment, discovery) self-government and other creative undertakings. Population planning keeps the numbers of people in balance with technology and resources. Rational efforts are made to keep age distributions in dynamic ratio—although the concept of "planned death" raises admittedly difficult problems. Machines take over labor functions almost entirely and leave people free to develop creative talents. Men are the masters; machines the responsive slaves. The boundary between "serious work" (more or less "productive" labor) and the serious hobby disappears. People do what they like to do—sail the seven seas in small boats, climb mountains, keep bees—without stigma of laziness or irresponsibility. People gain in freedom and individuality.

Pessimistic

Societies in which automation performs most of the functions and large numbers of human beings are left with time which they do not know how to spend. Proliferation of neuroses and alienations. Vast cities with enormous slums; people poorly fed, housed, educated and in ill-health. The old and young over-balanced in proportion to those of working age. Urban social, economic and political functions lag behind population growth and technology. Welfare programs inadequate; transportation hopelessly snarled.

Optimistic

Urban areas carefully and functionally planned to allow open spaces—mountains, lakes, beaches, parks, etc. Cities and open spaces blend. All wastes—water, air, food remnants, scrap metal—collected and reprocessed. Social services and public facilities (hospitals, universities, museums, art galleries, etc.) localized for access and community integration. Some cities, in themselves, become works of art.

Pessimistic

Disappearance of forests and wildlife, except in a few, inadequate reserves; vast stretches of tarmac, concrete paving and rows of prefabricated dwelling boxes. Continuing pollution of rivers, lakes, harbors, bays, coastal waters and air. Social services and public facilities scattered and inadequate for immense population.

Optimistic

Cybernetics, learning theory, teaching machines and general systems conceptual frameworks speed the learning process enormously to develop citizens who can adapt to the exponential growth of technology and participate in adjusting their social, economic and political institutions to a rapidly changing environment. The new learning fosters a renaissance in the arts. From this learning and as an outcome of wisdom accumulated from practical experience, an enlightened citizenry of the world will discover how to make constructive use of bioengineering, the prolongation of human life, and the capacity for creating life. The world becomes a pleasant place in which to live—material needs are adequately met, and the traditional terrors of early and violent death are virtually eliminated. People are free to pursue lives of deep satisfaction.

Pessimistic

Scientific and technological developments proceed so rapidly that only a narrow intellectual elite can keep up with exploding knowledge and specialized skills. Political, social and economic institutions increasingly fail in making adjustments to the changing environment, and individual human beings find it increasingly difficult to adapt psychologically and behaviorally to the changes that are taking place so rapidly. Either those relative few who master the new learning and technology control those who do not have access to knowledge and skills (or those who lack the ability to learn in a highly competitive environment); or, those who understand the uses of power win over or manipulate the skilled and knowledgeable elite and thereby rule the rank and file of the populace. For all but a favored few the world becomes an increasingly regimented and unpleasant place—and with time even the rulers may find themselves disagreeably constricted by growing populations and seemingly shrinking space.

A Basic Framework
for Social Science:
Two Fundamental Human-Earth
Equations and Their Juxtaposition

BY ROBERT A. HARPER

Teachers would generally agree that the basic task of the social studies is to give students an understanding of the world in which they live—not only the world of their personal lives, their families and communities, their country, but also of the larger world that lies behind the newspaper headlines and television news broadcasts. But the task of making sense out of a world in which three billion people live in a seemingly infinite variety of planetary variations is fantastically complex. What is most needed is some over-all frame of reference to bridge the gap between the individual's observable world and the more abstract planetary world.

The first step in providing an over-all framework is to look for the variables that are of major importance in explaining human activity whether at the local level or the global. The elements in the over-all equation we are seeking to identify are: (1) The nature of the individual; (2) the character of the group, society, or culture within which he lives; (3) the earth environment within which the group lives; (4) the technological capacity of the group to make use of the environmental and cultural resources; and (5) the interrelations between the group at its particular location on the earth and other places and peoples. All inquiry within the social studies would seem to deal with one or more of these elements; and, to a large extent, all analysis of major questions involves the interrelations among them.

But to understand the world in which we live, whether viewed at the close range of family and community or the longest range of planet Earth, we still must have an over-all frame that will give us understanding of the interrelationship between man and his environment. For, in its simplest form, the human problem has been and will remain—how to wrest the necessities of life from the environment. And from the dim beginnings of human existence this problem has been not only an individual matter but one for the larger group, the society.

The Traditional Man-Earth Equation

Throughout pre- and early history, man's capacity for understanding and working with the earth environment was so limited by his technology that the focus of not only the individual's attention but that of the group was highly localized. The group did not have a global range or even a continental range. The problem of living was to figure out how to sustain life on the particular part of real estate that the group occupied, and the basic human instrument for using the particular local environment was the collective capacity of the group as it developed by trial and error and inspiration over time.

A social science of the world of man throughout most of man's history, then, has been the study of the many different societies or cultural groups, each living in its own particular piece of earth real estate. Each group could be studied in itself or in terms of particular aspects of its life; or groups, or particular aspects of life, could be studied comparatively from group to group. In either case, the world appears like mosaic tiles, each to be studied in terms of the man-environmental conditions within the tiles or to be compared and contrasted with other tiles.

Of course, even before man left written records the individual man-earth tiles were not completely separate. Difficult as movement over the earth was to primitive man, remarkable journeys were made. Individuals and parties moved between groups; and while they couldn't carry much in the way of goods, there was a traffic in ideas and in particularly valuable commodities—seeds, plants, animals, and critical artifacts. But the inputs to any local community from outside, though often of fundamental significance, were still secondary to the basic problem of human life: how the group could wrest a better living from its distinctive earth environment.

Notice that we have established a basic conceptual framework for understanding human life on the earth. We have set down a descriptive model for relating the basic factors: individual, group, earth environment, technology, and interrelations between places. The frame makes more meaningful both the individual elements of the human equation and the interrelations that provide understanding of the whole. The task of analysis and description still is considerable, but there is a frame on which to build from the most minute ingredient in the over-all picture to a description of the whole.

The model of the equation of human life in the world that has just been described is readily recognized as one currently in vogue as an organizational frame for teaching the social sciences and social studies—the "cultural area" or "culture world" approach. It assumes the world to be divided into separate divisions on the basis of different culture groups; and it focuses on the fundamental problem of each group, which is to live off of its particular piece of earth real estate using the know-how that has been developed within the social group itself.

The analysis of each culture group in its own little world reveals many variations in the equation: different degrees of know-how, different group values, and different earth environments. Comparison of one group with another is most interesting, for all sorts of similarities and differences can be found in the solution to the problems of life: there are important similarities between groups living in very different earth environments; yet there are also important differences between groups in very similar earth environments. All facets of human life—value systems, economic activities, governmental organizations, social patterns—can be held up for comparative study.

Such a model of the human equation is basic to an understanding of the rationale of most of human history, and it is also fundamentally relevant to understanding a very large segment of the population of the earth today. Because, today, for much of mankind—in rural Asia, Latin America, and Africa and even in portions of Anglo-America, Europe and the Soviet Union—the problem of life remains a locally-oriented one. It is the earth environment within the local area—often within eyesight of home—that must provide almost all of the basic needs of life. And, despite greater and greater inputs of ideas and technology from the rest of the world, it is still the know-how of the local group—its culture and technology —that determines how the problem of the use of local environment will be attacked.

A Different Human Equation: The World-Wide Realm of Modern Life

The culture world approach has given us a model for understanding much of human history and a large segment of the earth's population today. Proponents of this approach to social sciences attribute its shortcomings to errors in teaching; not in the model itself. Thus, they chide us for our almost complete attention to only certain of the many culture worlds of man; namely, those of Western Man. Understanding of human relations will come, they infer, if we give "equal time" to other cultures.

But there is a fundamental difficulty in the culture world approach that cannot be solved by more attention to understanding the rationale of cultures other than our own, or even to more concern with comparison of different cultures. Large segments of today's world do not live according to the cultural-mosaic formula.

The model does not provide understanding of New York, London, Paris, Tokyo, Peiping, or even of the multitude of smaller urban communities in the world. None of these communities expects to support its population from the environmental resources of the local area.

For example, we cannot give students meaningful insight into the New York Metropolitan Area by describing the amount of high-rise office buildings built since World War II, counting the number of commuters entering Manhattan Island on a business day, or even describing the problems of ghetto life. Nor is New York today explicable even in terms of its people and their relations to the local resource base or the natural quality of the harbor, although even the promoters and builders of skyscrapers must take such matters into account.

New York must be seen for what it does rather than what it is—and it does much more than provide goods and services for its 15 million people. The banks and corporations with offices in those high towers are at the decision-making controls of two-way flows that, on the one hand, draw production from mines, plantations and farms, and factories at points throughout the world and, on the other hand, send finished goods and services not only throughout the United States but to centers in most parts of the world. The decisions of Standard Oil, Chase Manhattan Bank, J. C. Penney, Radio Corporation of America, and New York Life come from Manhattan's office towers, and they, multiplied by the more than 300 other major corporations and financial institutions headquartered in New York, have impact in Buffalo; Muncie, Indiana; Carbondale, Illinois; London; Tokyo; or Calcutta.

The lives, then, of most people in the United States, in Europe, or in the Soviet Union are tied into long-range connections that extend out from metropolitan centers such as New York. And, we cannot understand the agriculture of the U.S. Corn Belt, the Argentine Pampas, the Latin American or African coffee plantation, or even the collective farms of the Soviet Union in terms of man and land as in the closed-society model. The land as a resource base is essential to the system in terms of mass-production from parts of the world that appear to offer the best sources of particular commodities within limits of a particular political and economic organization. But the production decisions are made in terms of markets around the world and regularly implemented with capital from thousands of miles away.

It is the complex interconnections of this modern system that give meaning to big metropolitan centers such as New York City, small communities such as Carbondale, Illinois, or primary producing areas in Indiana, Florida, or the Australian grasslands.

Thus, there is a second very different man-earth equation in the world; one that had its origins in the limited inter-community contacts begun long ago and described as a secondary input factor in our local-base model. What made these contacts possible were long-range transportation and communication, enabling men to connect parts of the world separated by many miles. In the early stages of technology, caravan routes and, particularly, water routes—both river highways and the oceans—offered a possible alternative to the local-base solution to man's problem of living on the earth. For over these routes goods, ideas, and people could move from one particular culture-tile to another. However, because man's technology was so primitive, very little could actually be carried between locally-based communities by human porters, animals, wagons, or sail-powered vessels.

But the quantity of goods, people and ideas that could be moved long-distance were fantastically accelerated by the successive control and increased efficiency of inanimate energy sources—first water, then coal, petroleum, natural gas, and now nuclear energy—beginning with the Industrial Revolution 200 years ago. Later on the discovery of telegraph, telephone, radio, and TV reduced the time factor between places.

The revolutions in transportation and communications resulted in the model of the man-earth equation that began with the European sea empires and has spread to Anglo-America, to the Soviet Union, and is found in Japan, Australia, and in bridgeheads of cities and commercial producing areas in almost every country of the world. This model depends not on man-land relations within a local area but rather on connections with other centers in a regional and, increasingly, a world-wide network. More and more, this model assumes mass consumption by persons throughout the system and specialized production in particular points within the system. Thus, each producing area has the possibility of supplying consumers throughout the system and, in turn, the producers have the possibility of consuming goods from any other point in the system.

The system radically varies the human equations, for no longer is the population of a particular point in the system bound by the limitations either of (1) the character of the earth environment at that point as a base of support, or (2) the limitations of the thought and technology of the particular culture group. Theoretically, all peoples within the system can draw the best of goods and ideas from any other part of the world-wide network. Thus, points throughout the earth environment form the production base for the system, and the collective know-how of all persons in the system provides the capacity to increase the understanding of the environment and its possible use. Know-how and technology developing within the system even offer the possibility of expanding beyond the limitations of the earth's crust to draw on other bodies in space.

As we have noted, this new world-wide system for supporting human life did not spring forth full-grown in the twentieth century. We know it evolved from the past and developed primarily from the Western European culture world. Perhaps the Roman Empire was an early attempt at such a system, but the equation took effective form first, probably, in the British Empire. And while that empire connected producing areas on all continents, it really organized only a tiny fraction of the possible earth resources. Other European countries developed their own intercontinental networks on a smaller scale; and the United States, a modified form of the European culture, also developed its own version of the new interconnected system by organizing the varied resources of a continent into a functioning whole and by strengthening its ties to Europe as well. Today, other examples of the interconnected model on varying scales can be seen in the organization of the Soviet Union and Japan. To an important degree, each country in today's world is trying to develop its own national resources and at the same time to tie into the increasingly developing world-wide connections. Thus, just as there were many variations on the locally-based culture world model, so are there numerous forms of the long-range interconnected system.

It could be argued that the new interconnected model, with its long-range connections that now are increasingly of global proportions, is just a larger-scale version of the traditional model: modern transportation has simply extended the range of the human resource base; instead of a walking distance from a locality that range is now global. But there are other differences as well. Traditionally we have thought of the locally-based culture in terms of the organization of contiguous territory—the culture area, the political state, the economic region. But the British Empire with its connections across unoccupied seas presented the beginnings of point-to-point connections across gaps that were not a part of the system. Increasingly, the new interconnected system with its global scale is of that sort. Activity is centered more and more in giant metropolitan foci, and modern transportation and communication are primarily of a point-to-point nature connecting the metropolises.

The nature of the interconnected modern world is perhaps best characterized by jet air travel where the traveler boards a plane in one airport and is carried directly high into the sky above the clouds, where he no longer views the world unfolding in front of him as he has in all forms of conventional land transport; and, then, at his destination he drops down into another metropolitan center much like the one he left. Increasingly such experiences are not just those between metropolitan centers on a single continent but between centers throughout the world-wide intercontinental system.

The Two Equations in Social Science Teaching

Our world today is made up of two very different equations for human life on the earth: (1) the traditional locally-based culture which depends primarily on the know-how of a particular small group out of the total population of the earth and on the resources of a tiny fragment of the full earth environment, and (2) the new world-wide interconnected system that draws on the resources of parts of the whole earth and, we might add, is building its own distinctive culture by incorporating bits and pieces from the many different culture areas that it touches, although its European origins appear to be still dominant.

We have identified our task in social science as giving individuals an understanding of the world in which they live and, within that charge, to find order in the chaos of the myriad human and earth relations in a seemingly infinite number of places. Our aim is to find an over-all framework within which to examine the variations of human life over the world.

Fundamental to our task in providing understanding of human life on the earth today is something more than just that different human groups have developed variations on a single human equation of living on the earth; in fact, mankind today lives according to two systems that draw upon the earth environment in very different ways and result in fundamentally different perspectives of life and in very different problems and potentials.

The framework of social science should establish the two different human systems as the basic frame within which to compare and contrast life from place to place or component to component. Parts of the whole of mankind's life on the earth relate to one or the other or both of these two systems.

The two models we have outlined would seem to offer the basic ingredients of the over-all framework. All human life can be viewed as falling within one or the other of the two models. Thus, the frame of social science may be provided by the examination of the two models, their internal variations from place to place and culture to culture, and the juxtaposition of the two basic systems from one place to the other over the earth.

Surely the two systems impinge upon one another. As we have noted, no primarily locally-based community is completely isolated from contacts with the world-wide interconnected network. Someone from the interconnected system—doctor, missionary, or scientist—has entered the community. Eskimos drink tea and carry firearms; primitive Africans raise cotton to sell, or leave the village to work in mines. All of the centers of the world-wide network, not only have contacts today with some fundamentally locally-based communities, but, in fact, have developed out of locally-based communities of the past. Thus, they carry vestiges of locally-based values in their culture—political and social ideas, thoughts about what is "right" and "wrong," about God, about what to eat. The fact that we tend to teach social sciences emphasizing the "cultures of the world" approach, rather than of the two models of human life, is an indication of our locally-based tradition and of our view of a political state necessarily covering contiguous territory and expecting the primary loyalty of all peoples within that territory.

It might be thought that social scientists already recognize the two different systems and deal with them. We regularly talk of "developed" and "underdeveloped" areas, sometimes using other terms such as "industrial" and "nonindustrial" or "technologically advanced" and "technologically less-advanced." But such a division tends to follow the old mosaic-tile approach, separating the world into really homogeneous pieces.

The point is that the two different systems are not found side-by-side in the traditional mosaic pattern. Instead, the interconnected network has spread over the mosaic, touching down in particular points, but not in others. Thus, in any given part of the earth one can find the two different systems in close juxtaposition. In the Congo, most people may still live in the locally-based system focused on their own piece of earth real estate, but Leopoldville is a city with regular communication and traffic with the world-wide network as are the Katanga copper region and other producing areas. Mexico is both Mexico City, with its rather important position in the interconnected world, and the Indian village, which is only peripherally tied to the world beyond walking distance from the village. In the United States, at first glance, the whole country might be considered part of the interconnected network, but what about the Navajos or even the rural European stock in parts of Appalachia or the Ozarks?

It may appear that the two systems have been largely defined in economic terms. This is because the problem has been seen particularly in terms of two different approaches to how to live in this world, and living depends first of all upon a system of economic sustenance. But the two systems, as we know, in reality touch on all aspects of man's life. This is easy to see in the locally-based model. There the social group has been largely isolated; so it has had to work out all of the questions of life— what is right, as well as what to eat; what is the meaning of life, as well as what to wear.

The world-wide interconnected system is also more than just an economic system. There is developing something of a common culture within the system. For example, in communities throughout the system interest in jazz, in mini-skirts, or in *zen* or *yoga* is evidence of this.

The point is that the examination of social science in terms of the over-all frame of the two model systems and their juxtaposition gives us a base for understanding either the whole of mankind's life on this earth or of any part of it. It gives us a basis for not only comparison, but for comprehending pieces of the whole, whether those pieces involve either issues or areas. We can use the frame in developing the historical time-dimension as well as in examining the present scene. Within it we can study at any scale: that of the real world of the individual's everyday life at one extreme, and that of the abstract planetary world at the other.

The frame also enables us to examine the world at different levels of complexity. It would seem essential that any conceptual frame for social science be applicable at all levels of the individual's educational development— from nursery school to the Ph.D. Often the simplistic world we paint in the early grades is not just simple; it is an unreal myth that presents misconceptions that are most difficult to change. As a geographer, the example that comes to mind is the mental set caused by case studies of peoples living within different environmental zones of the earth—the tropical forests, deserts, or mid-latitude coasts—with the inference that differences in peoples are primarily the result of the different environmental circumstances they find themselves in. In the same way, early studies that concentrate on countries or cultures grossly misrepresent the situation.

The two-fold framework of human life is not simplistic. Analysis of either system is complex; and, as yet, we have little empirical data on the flow of information, of decision-making and control in the world-wide interconnected system. But we have been concerned with establishing real challenges within social sciences that will take hold of the best students, and the frame proposed here would seem to offer that challenge and at the same time provide a vehicle within which modern scientific techniques and tools can be applied to the social sciences.